QUEEN VICTORIA

Queen
Victoria

A Life of Contradictions

MATTHEW DENNISON

St. Martin's Press New York

QUEEN VICTORIA. Copyright © 2013 by Matthew Dennison.
All rights reserved. Printed in the United States of America. For
information, address St. Martin's Press,
175 Fifth Avenue, New York, N.Y. 10010.

www.stmartins.com

Library of Congress Cataloging-in-Publication Data

Dennison, Matthew.
    Queen Victoria : a life of contradictions / Matthew Dennison. —
First U.S. edition.
        p. cm.
    Includes bibliographical references and index.
    ISBN 978-1-250-04889-9 (hardcover)
    ISBN 978-1-4668-5001-9 (e-book)
    1. Victoria, Queen of Great Britain, 1819–1901. 2. Queens—Great
Britain—Biography. 3. Great Britain—History—Victoria, 1837–
1901—Biography. I. Title.
    DA554.D46 2014
    941.081092—dc23
    [B]

                                                    2014007562

St. Martin's Press books may be purchased for educational, business,
or promotional use. For information on bulk purchases, please contact
Macmillan Corporate and Premium Sales Department at 1-800-221-
7945, extension 5442, or write specialmarkets@macmillan.com.

First published in Great Britain by William Collins, an imprint of
HarperCollins Publishers

First U.S. Edition: June 2014

10 9 8 7 6 5 4 3 2 1

For Gráinne and Aeneas, with all love

'I could tell you my adventures – beginning from this morning,' said Alice a little timidly: 'but it's no use going back to yesterday, because I was a different person then.'

Lewis Carroll, *Alice's Adventures in Wonderland*, 1865

'Elizabeth [I] was a *great Queen* but a *bad woman*; and even in her royal capacity she erred sometimes; she had a very great idea of her prerogative and was more arbitrary even than her tyrannical father.'

Princess Victoria, *c*.1834

CONTENTS

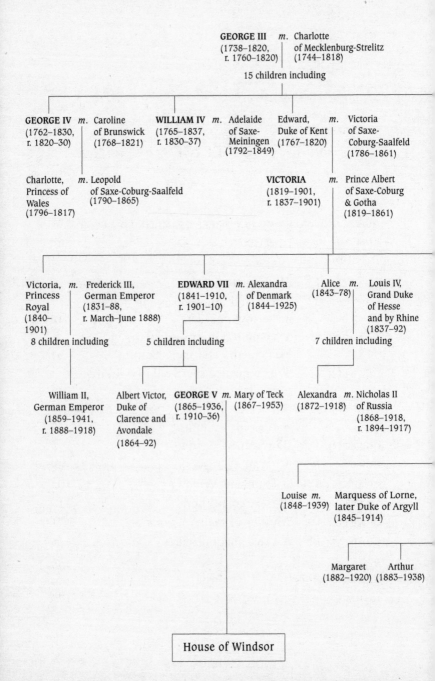

GEORGE III m. Charlotte
(1738–1820,   of Mecklenburg-Strelitz
r. 1760–1820)   (1744–1818)

15 children including

GEORGE IV m. Caroline   WILLIAM IV m. Adelaide   Edward,   m. Victoria
(1762–1830,   of Brunswick   (1765–1837,   of Saxe-   Duke of Kent   of Saxe-
r. 1820–30)   (1768–1821)   r. 1830–37)   Meiningen   (1767–1820)   Coburg-Saalfeld
                                                (1792–1849)   (1786–1861)

Charlotte,   m. Leopold   VICTORIA   m. Prince Albert
Princess of   of Saxe-Coburg-Saalfeld   (1819–1901,   of Saxe-Coburg
Wales   (1790–1865)   r. 1837–1901)   & Gotha
(1796–1817)   (1819–1861)

Victoria,   m. Frederick III,   EDWARD VII m. Alexandra   Alice   m. Louis IV,
Princess   German Emperor   (1841–1910,   of Denmark   (1843–78)   Grand Duke
Royal   (1831–88,   r. 1901–10)   (1844–1925)   of Hesse
(1840–   r. March–June 1888)   and by Rhine
1901)   (1837–92)

8 children including   5 children including   7 children including

William II,   Albert Victor,   GEORGE V m. Mary of Teck   Alexandra m. Nicholas II
German Emperor   Duke of   (1865–1936,   (1867–1953)   (1872–1918)   of Russia
(1859–1941,   Clarence and   r. 1910–36)   (1868–1918,
r. 1888–1918)   Avondale   r. 1894–1917)
                   (1864–92)

                                                                Louise m. Marquess of Lorne,
                                                                (1848–1939) later Duke of Argyll
                                                                             (1845–1914)

                                                                Margaret   Arthur
                                                                (1882–1920) (1883–1938)

House of Windsor

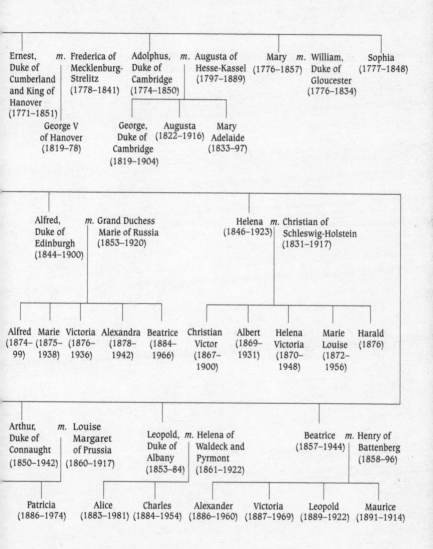

Queen Victoria's
Family Tree:
A Simplified Version

Ernest, *m.* Frederica of   Adolphus, *m.* Augusta of   Mary *m.* William,   Sophia
Duke of   Mecklenburg-   Duke of   Hesse-Kassel   (1776–1857) Duke of   (1777–1848)
Cumberland   Strelitz   Cambridge   (1797–1889)   Gloucester
and King of (1778–1841)   (1774–1850)   (1776–1834)
Hanover
(1771–1851)

            George V   George,   Augusta   Mary
            of Hanover   Duke of   (1822–1916) Adelaide
            (1819–78)   Cambridge   (1833–97)
                                 (1819–1904)

        Alfred,   *m.* Grand Duchess   Helena *m.* Christian of
        Duke of   Marie of Russia   (1846–1923) Schleswig-Holstein
        Edinburgh   (1853–1920)   (1831–1917)
        (1844–1900)

Alfred   Marie   Victoria Alexandra Beatrice   Christian   Albert   Helena   Marie   Harald
(1874–   (1875–   (1876–   (1878–   (1884–   Victor   (1869–   Victoria   Louise   (1876)
99)   1938)   1936)   1942)   1966)   (1867–   1931)   (1870–   (1872–
                                                    1900)   1948)   1956)

Arthur,   *m.* Louise   Leopold, *m.* Helena of   Beatrice *m.* Henry of
Duke of   Margaret   Duke of   Waldeck and   (1857–1944) Battenberg
Connaught   of Prussia   Albany   Pyrmont   (1858–96)
(1850–1942)   (1860–1917)   (1853–84)   (1861–1922)

    Patricia   Alice   Charles   Alexander   Victoria   Leopold   Maurice
    (1886–1974)   (1883–1981) (1884–1954) (1886–1960) (1887–1969) (1889–1922) (1891–1914)

LIST OF ILLUSTRATIONS

LIST OF ILLUSTRATIONS

Introduction

On the eve of Queen Victoria's coronation, in June 1838, Charles Greville committed to his diary a memorable description of the capital. 'It is as if the population had been on a sudden quintupled; the uproar, the confusion, the crowd, the noise, are indescribable. Horsemen, footmen, carriages squeezed, jammed, intermingled . . . not a mob here and there but the town all mob . . . the park one vast encampment . . . and still the roads are covered, the railroads loaded with arriving multitudes.'[1] Remove the horses and Greville's picture is recognisable to the modern reader familiar with London in the grip of royal fervour. *The Times* attempted to unravel the attitude of Greville's 'mob': 'They thought of [Victoria] not as an individual to be loved with headlong zeal or played upon by corrupt adulation . . . they regarded her as in herself *an institution.*'[2] Victoria's success over the course of a long reign was to unite, to the benefit of both, the individual and the institution. In a very personal sense, the monarchy became 'Victorian': in the minds of many of Victoria's subjects, the throne acquired what they understood as her own virtues. This symbiosis invested the British Crown with a tangibly human aspect at the same time as exalting

Victoria herself as an archetype and exemplar of all that was laudable in a woman and a ruler. It was partly good fortune, partly born of a sympathetic popular mindset shaped by culture and economics. As we shall see, Victoria's behaviour did not consistently merit approbation, which, throughout her final decades and beyond, came close to idolatry.

Hers did not begin as a cult of personality: that happened later. From infancy those closest to her schooled her in a course of exemplary behaviour: her mother, her governess, her canny Uncle Leopold. A backlash against the burlesque and buffoonery of her immediate predecessors, their model of rectitude encouraged a suppression of self in the interests of a tarnished Crown. Outwardly, Victoria's monarchy came to be characterised by probity, continence and earnestness, all 'Victorianisms' derided by posterity. Yet this mandate of good behaviour provided an imprimatur of some resilience for a throne that, in political terms, continued to lose ground to an increasingly elected and representative Parliament. If Victoria did not always keep faith with that mandate, she mostly avoided publishing her transgressions. Returning to the fray at the time of her death, *The Times* was able to assert unblushingly that, if the monarchy stood 'broad-based upon the people's will . . . we owe these results, to a degree which is hardly possible to over-estimate, to the womanly sweetness, the gentle sagacity, the utter disinteredness, and the unassailable rectitude of the Queen'.[3]

Readers of the following account of Victoria's life will discover that her sweetness, sagacity, disinteredness and rectitude were all variable qualities: she was a woman of dizzying contradictions and myriad inconsistencies, but deeply etched in her makeup was a towering wilfulness that intermittently rendered her foolish, selfish, blinkered, exasperating and apparently self-destructive. In virtually the same breath she was capable of immense charm, humility, compassion, candour, perspicacity, generosity, intrepidity and understanding. 'How sadly deficient I am, and how over-sensitive and irritable, and how uncontrollable my temper is when annoyed and hurt,' she confessed to her journal on New Year's Day 1881.[4] She was unflinchingly honest throughout her life, especially with herself. Repeatedly that honesty failed to equate with accurate self-knowledge. A surer estimate than that of *The Times* belongs to her last prime minister, Lord Salisbury, who commended her 'inflexible conscience' and 'unflagging industry'. Neither predisposition shaped her conduct life long.

She did not read Walter Bagehot's *The English Constitution*, published in 1867. Even without that guidance – staple reading for her successors – she insisted to ministers and prime ministers, clergymen, generals, foreign statesmen and rulers, as well as her own family, on her rights to be consulted, to encourage and to warn, and did so with vehemence and some success. A reluctant showman, she is unlikely to have embraced Bagehot's definition of public life as akin to theatre: 'the climax of the play is the Queen'.[5] By the end of her reign, however, she had convincingly overturned his qualification that 'nobody supposes that their house is like the court; their life like her life; her orders like their orders'. Not least among Victoria's achievements was her calculated presentation of herself as an acme of ordinariness. Even as she exulted in the riches and grandeur of empire, she appeared Britain's first middle-class monarch, her way of life recognisable and, for the most part, comprehensible to the vast mass of her subjects. Moreover she did so on an international stage, so that the woman who was herself so preoccupied with British prestige abroad became in time a chief source of the very prestige she valued so highly.

Victoria believed in commemoration. She cheated death's sting by celebrating those taken from her in concrete and enduring form. She in turn inspired similar acts of conspicuous memorialising and rightly remains among Britain's best-known and most visible monarchs. So extensive are surviving primary sources relating to her life and reign that it is possible, as academics and biographers have discovered, to support divergent and conflicting interpretations. The present, deliberately short account of Victoria's life is necessarily a selective portrait. It encompasses aspects of her private and public worlds, of her internal as well as her external landscapes. None is exhaustive, though the focus is consistently Victoria herself: my aim has not been to offer a vision of the age, of her marriage, her family, her legacy. Rather, in attempting to capture what I consider telling aspects of this enduringly great Briton, I hope the present account arrives at a pithy but illuminating definition of its own, albeit qualified and circumscribed by the restrictions of its format.

1

'Pocket Hercules'

In the spring of 1819, Britain's royal family lacked heirs in the third generation. None denied the fecundity of the geriatric King and his recently deceased queen. George III – mad, irascible, tearful and, to a host of unglimpsed imaginary listeners, still talkative despite his deafness – and red-nosed, snuff-sniffing, cricket-loving Charlotte of Mecklenburg-Strelitz (plain-featured even in likenesses by Gainsborough and Allan Ramsay) had produced fifteen children and a template of royal domesticity which, with dire consequences, discounted cosiness or intimacy between parents and children. Their vigorous momentum had not been maintained. Too many of those children remained unmarried – or sloppily embroiled in the rouged embrace of middle-aged mistresses, childless or giving birth only to bastards and ill repute; the babble and patter of grandchildren scarcely touched the sovereigns' dotage. So easily did bad parenting come close to extinguishing a dynasty.

The Prince Regent, future George IV, was the eldest of the fifteen: in his late fifties balloon-faced, extravagant and quick to pique. Married at the wish of his parents and Parliament, he was father to a single daughter. Like the Regent's mother another Charlotte, she ought in time to have become Queen of England. Instead she died in 1817 giving birth to a stillborn son. Her short life had been one of shoddy rambunctiousness. Her loathsome parents loathed one another. Neither scrupled to shield their daughter from their differences. In the circumstances this apple-cheeked girl of novelettish instincts might have turned out worse – born of the loveless coupling of a prodigal sybarite and a hoydenish German princess slap-dash in the cleanliness of her undergarments and after-wards, it was claimed, over-generous with her favours. In retrospect Charlotte appears a quintessentially Regency figure.

The unnecessary death of the King's granddaughter and only heiress presumptive, attributed to obstetric malpractice, had provoked nationwide grief and a crisis in the monarchy. 'In the dust/ the fair-haired daughter of the isles is laid,/ the love of millions,' Byron lamented. Commemorative cups and saucers, cream jugs, even printed handkerchiefs echoed the strain. With incontinent capitalisation, one broadsheet implored the nation to, 'Reflect upon the Uncertainty of HUMAN LIFE, So strikingly exemplified in THE DEATH Of your amiable and much lamented PRINCESS', a didactic imperative which anticipates the lugubrious piety of the remainder of the century. Politician Henry Brougham described public reaction 'as though every household throughout Great Britain had lost a favourite child'. Belatedly remorseful – and too late for Charlotte, of course – the hapless obstetrician Sir Richard Croft shot himself. The princess's death did not inspire her woebegone father once more unto the breach: at forty-nine, the vilified Princess of Wales would not produce a second heir.

That task fell instead to the Regent's six surviving younger brothers: Frederick, William, Edward, Ernest,

Augustus and Adolphus, in Shelley's estimation the 'dregs of their dull race'. Mired in debt and bawdy, these flaunting adulterers were lethargic in matters of duty, slatternly and discreditable, tarnished to the extent of accusations of incest and murder – a boon to caricaturists: with their wigs, pockmarks, gluttony and gout not even ornamental. With hindsight they would be regarded as a nadir for Britain's monarchy, 'a race of small German breast-bestarred wanderers', as anti-monarchist MP Charles Bradlaugh later described the Hanoverians.[1] For the high-minded if alarmist Prince Albert, they would provide an enduring cautionary tale.

Of the seven possible progenitors in the aftermath of Charlotte's death, William, Edward and Adolphus responded to the siren call of a regal vacancy and an anxious Parliament prepared to barter their debts for an heir (Frederick and Ernest were already married). Hastily they allied themselves to a trio of uninspiring Protestant German princesses: all lacked even the misplaced high spirits of the Regent's estranged wife. In April 1819, it was Adolphus's wife, Augusta, Duchess of Cambridge, who gave birth to a healthy son. He was christened George. For seven weeks this infant prince of Cambridge was alone eligible in his generation to inherit the throne of England. But Adolphus was the youngest of the married brothers. Senior in precedence were William, Duke of Clarence (later William IV), described after his death as 'not . . . a prince of brilliant and commanding talents';[2] Edward, Duke of Kent, of martinet stiffness, black-dyed hair, surprising philanthropy and tender-hearted devotion to his bride; and Ernest, Duke of Cumberland: emaciated, charmless and acerbic, but more sensitive than history has allowed to his status as England's most hated man.

And so from the outset Alexandrina Victoria of Kent was a person of consequence. Born as dawn broke over the southeast corner of Kensington Palace on 24 May 1819, in a room whose costly refurbishment her fifty-one-year-old father had completed only two days previously, she immediately displaced her Cambridge cousin in the line of succession. Sources disagree on when she herself first learnt it. An aura of consequence – occasionally cultivated, occasionally insisted upon – was an attribute she would never lose.

She would become one of England's most vigorous monarchs. As a baby, her father described her as 'a model of strength': 'more of a pocket Hercules, than a pocket Venus'.[3] Perhaps something of the urgency and precariousness of that scramble which preceded her birth remained with her life long. It is discernible in her later conviction of her own eminence, her retreat behind that impenetrable shield, 'Queen of England': she may not have forgotten that her queenship was so nearly that of her older cousin, Charlotte, or indeed young George. At different levels, hers is the response of the lottery-winning poor relation and, at the same time, simply one manifestation of a remarkably forceful nature. Over time much of her public life, with its parade of accessible virtues, represented a deliberate revision of the indignity of her pre-history and the tattered record of her immediate forebears. Fanciful to claim that she was born to right the record: her selfishness and sense of entitlement were equal to those of any of her father's siblings. But guided by those nearest to her, and prompted by the memory of uncles and aunts set on lives of eighteenth-century excess, as well as her own impulsive if inconsistent craving to exploit her position for good, she would redefine the face and function of British monarchy. She embraced an outlook some have labelled middle class and did so with wholehearted sincerity, as much a stranger to real middle-class mores as she was to those of the aristocracy she mistrusted or the Highland tenantry she determinedly idealised. Victoria's reign reasserted – and successfully bequeathed to her successors – what her contemporary Mrs Oliphant described as 'that tradition of humdrum virtue' established by her grandfather George III:[4] in that respect she became in fact as well as appearance, as Lady Granville described her in her infancy, *'le roi Georges* in petticoats'.[5]

'Plump as a partridge', this child whom J. M. Barrie memorialised in *Peter Pan in Kensington Gardens* as 'the most celebrated baby of the Gardens'[6] emerged into a world of confinement. That too would persist life long. Although as queen, Victoria flexed her muscles constitutionally and unconstitutionally and was not averse to threatening abdication when it suited her, she never with any conviction sought to escape her restrictive destiny. Her status as queen defined her in her own eyes: it was she who bandied the title *'doyenne* of sovereigns', its unnuanced orotundity indicative of her later complacency. Sovereignty was in two senses her legacy from her father, for the Duke of Kent was not only royal but romantic too. He had accepted without question the gypsy prophecy told to him on Malta that his unborn child would become a great queen. History has frequently agreed.

For all his dreaming, her father was injudicious. His frequent good intentions – his scheme to educate the sons of the military and his support for Catholic emancipation, for example – could not outweigh that half-crazy disciplinarianism which caused gossiping diarist and

Clerk to the Privy Council, Charles Greville, to dismiss him as 'the greatest rascal that ever went unhung'.[7] His duchess too was not clever. Society labelled her a stupid foreigner, 'the most mediocre person it would be possible to meet'.[8] Ditto the woman who in 1824 became Victoria's governess, a caraway seed-chewing Hanoverian Lutheran of sharp features and sharper self-estimation called Louise Lehzen. Both women were singularly determined, invested in good measure with the instinct for survival, the one spikily conscious of rank, the other given to jaundice, headaches and nervous debilitation; equal in their firmness and jealously exacting. Determination and adamantine self-will became enduring characteristics of their charge, successfully checked by neither. Lehzen at least made Victoria's wellbeing her lodestar. Her reward was love and, for an interlude, a front row seat in her pupil's unfolding drama.

Victoire, Duchess of Kent was a striking-looking widow of assured if showy dress sense, pink-cheeked and garrulous, but slow to master English with confidence. Until his death in 1814, her unappealing first husband, Charles Emich of Leiningen, had ruled without distinction, or the appearance of common sense, a territory in Lower Franconia much depleted by Napoleon. Leiningen's dark-haired widow, allied to Edward, Duke of Kent in 1818, as England still reeled from Princess Charlotte's death, quitted Germany with a son and daughter of pleasing aspect, Charles and Feodore; she took with her too the memory of financial hardship and emotional neglect. Her second marriage offered no respite from the former and so acquired a peripatetic character, husband and wife constantly travelling in the interests of economy. Happily the Duke of Kent, whose governorship of Gibraltar in 1802, described as a 'reign of terror',[9] included sentencing

a man to a flogging of 900 lashes,[10] regarded his duchess
unequivocally as 'a young and charming Princess'[11] and
implored her quite sincerely to 'love me as I love you'.[12]
For just this happiness had he set aside his kind and
comfortable mistress of three decades, Julie de St Laurent
– that and the hope that Parliament would increase his
allowance handsomely. (Parliament decided otherwise,
happy to act shabbily.) Since the Duke died of pneumonia,
reputedly caught from wet boots, on 23 January 1820 –
on an extended sojourn to the seaside at Sidmouth, which
offered bracing sea breezes at modest rates – Alexandrina
Victoria cannot have remembered her parents' wedded
bliss: she was eight months old. Their happiness found
reflections in her own spectacularly loving marriage. In
the meantime, she grew up to share the sentiments of her
aunt, Elizabeth, Landgravine of Hesse-Homburg, that her
parents' 'domestic comfort . . . broke up' was 'a very sad,
sad thing'.[13]

Infancy prevented her from recognising that atmosphere of petty contentiousness which hung, like the odour
of penury, about the large apartment in Kensington
Palace. No public rejoicing greeted her birth: like his
brothers, her father was not popular. Superstitious and
in the throes of a late-in-life infatuation with his much
younger wife, the Duke of Kent may have been convinced
that *his* daughter was a sovereign-in-waiting – as Edith
Sitwell described her, 'conceived, born and bred . . . to
mount the summits of greatness';[14] he was wise enough
mostly to disguise that hope. 'I should deem it the height
of presumption to believe it probable that a future heir
to the Crown of England would spring from me,' he
asserted with questionable frankness.[15] More sober coun-
sels, the Regent among them, anticipated an heir from
the Duke of Clarence and his whey-faced young bride

Adelaide of Saxe-Meiningen, whose first child had died only two months earlier within hours of her birth (the first of four disappointments for the long-suffering Clarences). Like the Clarences themselves, they would be thwarted in that expectation. The Regent feigned boredom at the princess's birth, but true to his nature of petulant caprice, the following month roused himself to sufficient rancour to spoil her christening. He changed her parents' preferred name of Victoire Georgiana Alexandrina Charlotte Augusta to Alexandrina Victoria: the unwieldy, foreign-sounding 'Alexandrina' was a tribute to the baby's most powerful sponsor, Alexander I of Russia, who would play no part in her upbringing. By striking out Charlotte and the feminine form of his own name, the Regent symbolically denied the baby's connection to himself and any claim to the throne. He also held at arm's length the niece in whom he took no interest. The Duchess of Clarence, by contrast, wrote to her affectionately on her third birthday as 'dear little Xandrina Victoria':[16] abbreviation came quickly. For much of her childhood she was simply 'Drina'. On her accession 'Alexandrina' would be dropped entirely, although a bill of 1831 to change the child's name by Act of Parliament to Charlotte Victoria had proved unsuccessful. It was a matter in which the twelve-year-old Victoria had no say: later she was grateful for its outcome, which freed her somewhat from the shadow of her cousin and her grandmother. Victoria assuredly owed her crown to her cousin's death: an egotist in terms of her royal role (if not in all matters), she sought to cast her reign in no one's image but her own. Besides, she felt, her mother reported, a 'great attachment' to her second name, notwithstanding that unEnglishness and lack of British royal precedent which so troubled her uncle

William.[17] Later she would castigate Charlotte – alongside Elizabeth – as one of 'the ugliest "housemaids" names I ever knew'.[18]

Foolish she may have been, unfortunate too in the mortality of her husbands: Victoria's mother possessed another significant attribute. She had been born Princess Marie Louise Victoire of Saxe-Coburg-Saalfeld. Charlotte's tragedy thus touched the Duchess of Kent closely for the women were sisters-in-law, Charlotte's husband Victoire's younger brother Leopold. Like parvenus in pursuit of ton, the ambitious and good-looking Coburgs were a family eager for greatness, none more so than Leopold. In coming decades Coburgers would colonise the palaces of Europe: their winning formula was a combination of dashing sex appeal, force of will and a self-serving phlegmatism in matters religious and political. Not without reason did Bismarck later vilify them as the 'stud-farm of Europe' or a Habsburg archduke complain that 'the Coburgs gain throne after throne and spread their growing power abroad over the whole earth'.[19] With Charlotte and her baby dead, and Leopold's dream of kingship by proxy in shreds, their second bite of the cherry fell to Victoire. It was Leopold who, as early as 1816, had drawn to the Duke of Kent's attention his lovely, lonely sister; Leopold who afterwards with renewed zeal encouraged Kent's hopes through a protracted courtship; Leopold who, metaphorically at least, hovered at his sister's shoulder. Kent's death was not the disaster Charlotte's had been, since his daughter survived him. It was Leopold who steadied Victoire's resolve as she grappled with her second bereavement.

Leopold also assisted his sister financially (though hardly to the top of his considerable means) and inspired her with dreams of glittering prizes and heavy-duty good advice; he insisted that she and the child live in Britain, albeit isolated and virtually friendless. As time would show, her compliance was enthusiastic. As keenly aware of the value of her trump card as any hard-bitten gamester, chary of her prerogatives and fully set upon the exercise of power, Victoire of Kent would prove tenacious in pursuit of the Coburg usurpation. But she played her hand badly. The Coburger who ruled England was neither Leopold nor his sister Victoire, who spent long years at variance with her daughter, but their nephew Albert, a case of third time lucky. In Albert's case, the Coburg will to power was balanced by a contradictory impulse, the 'Coburg melancholy'; both would leave their imprint.

Hostage to his own mismanagement, the Duke of Kent bequeathed his wife an impressive list of creditors and a decidedly unimpressive jointure of less than £300 a year. After her five-night vigil at her dying husband's bedside, the Duchess was unable to meet the costs of transporting his coffin to Windsor or herself and her daughter to London. It sounds a farcical impasse: it was certainly an inauspicious beginning to baby Victoria's august career. Unavoidably, mother and daughter remained for several weeks in Sidmouth, scene of their unhappiness, awaiting Leopold's help. Parliament granted the Duchess a royal widow's pension of £6,000, a modest sum by royal standards. As we will see, the Duke's own final gift to his wife also ultimately proved inadequate, though the Duchess was slow to recognise it: an egregiously venturesome helpmeet condemned by posterity.

John Conroy (from 1827 Sir John Conroy) was the Duke of Kent's equerry and one of his executors; following the Duke's death he became Comptroller of the Duchess's household. He exercised authority over her finances and her aspirations. For this hook-nosed Anglo-Irish landowner of severely limited means possessed unlimited ambition and a degree of swaggering magnetism. Gossips including no less a figure than the Duke of Wellington branded him the Duchess's lover: certainly theirs became an *egoïsme à deux*, which was itself an approach to intimacy. Conroy was a gambler with fate. He pinned his hopes on Victoria becoming queen and himself exercising power through the Duchess. Had he preferred the moonshine of dreams to the hard manipulation of scheming, he might have survived for future generations as a romantic figure. But he conceived of lasting benefits deriving first from the Duke of Kent's death, afterwards from Victoria's eminence. Inevitably over the next two decades he overplayed his hand. He earned Victoria's lasting enmity and, like the majority of the vanquished, forfeited the opportunity of telling his side of the story. Misguidedly he encouraged the Duchess in a course of behaviour towards her daughter which cost her Victoria's trust, her respect and, most importantly, her love.

Seeds sown by this predatory Irish adventurer were never harvested: Victoire did not steer the ship of state, even as Regent, and Conroy was prevented from basking in reflected glory. Victoria herself dismissed him from her household on her very first day as queen – after some delays pensioned off lucratively if with an ill grace. It was surely the right course of action. But for her father's death and Conroy's ambitions, Victoria's childhood might have been happier. Certainly the series of sketches of her at three years old made by Lady Elizabeth Keith Heathcote during a seaside holiday in Ramsgate suggest a normal toddler happy at normal toddler pursuits.[20] She was a healthy, active child, successfully inoculated against smallpox at the age of ten weeks. Breast-fed by her mother and cared for by her nurse Mrs Brock, she was contented, plump and wilful with the unyielding egotism of the very young, 'a greater darling than ever, but . . . beginning to show symptoms of wanting to get her own little way' as early as January 1820.[21] With few intermissions, she would remain plump and wilful. Thanks to her mother's sense of destiny, her infant world was as English as the German Duchess could make it (save for her German half-sister Feodore, her German governess Lehzen and the German lady-in-waiting, Baroness Späth, in attendance on her mother: a fluttering, unattractive, devoted woman widely written off as negligible and eventually expelled by Conroy). In 1822, mother and daughter sat together for William Beechey. In Beechey's portrait the exotic good looks belong to Victoria's German mother. For her part, Victoria is a generic English child, cherubic, blonde-haired and blue-eyed, as novelist Walter Scott remembered her at nine. In one chubby hand she clutches a miniature of her father. The habit of visible mourning, and of defining herself through her relationship to a deceased male, began early.

'When I think of His poor Miserable Wife, and His innocent, Fatherless Child, it really breaks my heart,' wrote the Duke of Kent's eldest unmarried sister Princess Augusta two days after the Duke's death in 1820.[22] The following week George III also died. Victoria's childhood would indeed come to include an element of broken-heartedness; happiness came afterwards. For the rest of her life there would be a series of surrogate father figures, including her uncle Leopold, her first prime minister and her husband. And in her friendships with women, even her own daughters, too often a reserve, occasionally hostility. The origin of both impulses is easy to trace: a childhood environment of querulous femininity and, with the exception of the exceptionable Conroy, male absence.

2

'Fresh and innocent as the flowers in her own garden'

ROOKS NESTED IN Kensington Gardens during Victoria's childhood: only in 1880, with the destruction of a grove of 700 elm trees, did they depart.[1] There were nuthatches among the beeches and horse chestnuts, jays too. To the passer-by it was a sylvan place, site of that 'country' palace acquired by William III and enriched by George I, '[full] of memories and legends; of notable or fantastic figures of the past'.[2] Two centuries ago, Kensington Palace was recognisably that 'pleasant place, surrounded by beautiful gardens, [in which] a little girl was brought up by her loving mother', imagined with a heavy dollop of syrup by children's author E. Nesbit in 1897.[3] 'Her teachers instructed her in music and languages, in history and all the things that children learn at school,' Nesbit told readers of *Royal Children of English History*. 'Her mother taught her goodness and her duty. There she grew up fresh and innocent as the flowers in her own garden, living a secluded life, like a princess in an enchanted palace.'

In Victoria's own version of her childhood, in which memories of the struggle against Conroy and the Duchess tinctured her picture of the whole, her secluded life included little enchantment. 'I led a very unhappy life as a child,' she would write to her eldest daughter in 1858:[4] her current state, as queen, wife and mother, quick to command, reluctant to be instructed, was infinitely preferable to those years of conflict. Not for her the poet's claim on her behalf that, 'She only knew her childhood's flowers/ Were happier pageantries!'[5] Nearly forty years on, careful to avoid excessive censure of her mother, she attributed that unhappiness to loneliness. She described herself as '[having] no scope for my very violent feelings of affection – [I] had no brothers and sisters to live with – never had had a father – from my unfortunate circumstances was not on a comfortable or at all intimate or confidential feeling with my mother . . . and did not know what a happy domestic life was!' Free from the shackles of filial piety, the historian need apportion blame less sparingly. And yet the Duchess of Kent was not deliberately the villainess she can all too easily be made to appear. She later attributed her erroneous ways to thoughtlessness, 'believing blindly, . . . [and] acting without reflexion'.[6]

Her position was not conducive to confidence. Beyond the spangled purlieus of the court of George IV, there was a ramshackle bravado to London in the first decades of the nineteenth century. Barrack-room bawdy and lusty xenophobia found vigorous expression in a popular culture of splenetic irreverence. Caricaturists targeted the royal family: their sex lives, their gargantuan appetites, their overspending, their all-pervasive folly. Short of money, friends and affection, dependent on the good will and handouts of her brother Leopold, and the tolerance of the new King, which was grudging in the extreme, the Duchess of Kent lacked a champion. She did not look far to fill the vacancy.

Conroy was an accomplished flirt. An indifferent soldier, he owed something of his military advancement to assiduous courtship of commanding officers' wives. His relationship with the plaintive royal widow is unlikely to have extended to a full-scale sexual liaison: from the outset the Duchess rated too highly her probable future as queen mother. Conroy's approach to the mistress whose experience of happy marriage had been so fleeting was at best manipulative, at worst bullying: she apologised to him on one occasion for being 'just an old stupid goose'.[7] A foxy sort of sexiness undoubtedly leavened his tough love, as did the same line in dark-hued melodrama which also won him the affection of the Duke of Kent's youngest surviving sister Princess Sophia, a neighbour at Kensington Palace: Conroy exploited the unmarried princess of failing eyesight without scruple as an easy source of ready cash and delved deep into her purse. But while he delighted Sophia with gossip,[8] he kept the Duchess on tenterhooks by stoking that paranoia to which the uncertainty of her position so easily tended. Her response was equally myopic. Victoria herself claimed later that Conroy had unnerved her mother with conspiracy theories centred on the wickedest of her wicked uncles, Ernest, Duke of Cumberland. Since Victoria stood between the throne and Cumberland, the Duke *must* be hellbent on her removal. It was strong meat, to rational minds perhaps too strong, as luridly coloured as contemporary lampoons, credible only within the context of what Leopold had described as 'a family whose members hate one another with an inconceivable bitterness'.[9] Like all Conroy's schemes, it aimed at isolating the Duchess and her daughter from their royal relatives. While the steely Irishman with the cleft chin and, in his portraiture, a suggestion of sardonic disdain in those hooded dark eyes, prevented anyone else from usurping his own position of influence, he appeared in the guise of protector. As if to confirm Conroy's whisperings, George IV stonily ignored the fledgling household in Kensington.

The Duchess's dread of her husband's family grew. When George IV did invite mother and daughter to Windsor, in 1826, she was convinced that the ageing monarch – corseted, enamelled, bewigged and panting – intended to kidnap Victoria. Stubbornly she defended the princess's seclusion. Over time she justified her line as shielding Victoria from her uncles' moral degeneracy. If her policy were immoderate – surely, in preventing Victoria from attending the coronation of William IV and 'poor *wishy-washy*' Queen Adelaide, as the latter's doctor described her, she overreached herself – we understand something of her anxiety. She forbade the company of cousins too, including George of Cambridge and George of Cumberland, contemporaries of equal rank; only Sir John's daughters, Victoire and Jane Conroy, were sanctioned as playmates. Unsurprisingly Victoria learnt to hate them. Instead she drew emotional sustenance from Lehzen. Companionship proved more elusive. Long hours she beguiled with an extensive collection of elaborately dressed wooden dolls. Velvet- and satin-primped ciphers of an imaginary world in which she existed autonomously and among friends, they represented an alternative reality – inspired by history lessons and those performances of bel canto opera at the King's Theatre in the Haymarket, which became a sole legitimate outlet for all her pent-up Hanoverian emotionalism: the young Victoria was stage-struck, in love with dancers and singers. Easy to discern a symbolic dimension to the Duchess's grey parrot: sharp-beaked, dingy-hued and prone to repeating confidences. More satisfactory a playmate was the spaniel

Dash with whom Sir George Hayter painted Victoria in 1835: until Victoria adopted him, he too had belonged to the Duchess, a present from Conroy.

In truth she was never alone. Central to what Leopold deplored as 'the Kensington system' devised by Conroy were constant shadowing and surveillance. The princess was not permitted to walk downstairs without someone holding her hand; the diary she began in 1832 was submitted to her mother's inspection (and correction); her public appearances were minutely directed and restricted to the extent that even *The Times* questioned her physical fitness, repeating rumours of disability; at night she slept in her mother's bedroom. Little wonder that Feodore, who in 1828 escaped to marry a landless princeling she had met twice, remembered these as 'years of imprisonment'. (For Victoria, further isolation and even cruelty would follow Feodore's departure.) Notable among the long-term effects of the Duchess's cocooning was 'Vickelchen's' need always to be the person of first consequence and an ever more determined self-will. Happily for her, both were outcomes her future role assured, though neither ought to be considered prerequisites. By the time Victoria in her turn sought to entrap her own daughters at her side, her motive personal convenience, Feodore was dead, unable to point out the irony.

Before queenship, an education. In April 1823, one month short of her fourth birthday, Victoria received her first instruction from the Reverend George Davys, a Lincolnshire clergyman of low-key Toryism and unassertive evangelism: basic skills of literacy and numeracy and the discreet but firm erasure of that trace of a German accent which the child had inevitably acquired.[10] 'I was not fond of learning as a little child,' she remembered later, 'and baffled every attempt to teach me my letters up to 5 years old – when I consented to learn them by their being written down before me.'[11] Victoria's reluctance notwithstanding, Davys's advent spelt the beginning of a programme of learning which would become a source of pride for the Duchess, and for her daughter the means by which, with careful stage-management, she discovered her splendid destiny.

Although the Duchess's household was sworn to silence concerning Vickelchen's future role, she could never have doubted that hers was a lofty station. Addressed as 'Your Royal Highness' from earliest infancy, she was attended out of doors by a liveried footman and her donkey rides in the palace gardens attracted the curiosity of passing crowds; she noticed the greater degree of respect accorded to her than to her twelve-years senior half-sister Feodore. 'There was no doubt that every care was taken to avoid premature disclosures,' her son-in-law Lord Lorne wrote in *VRI: Her Life and Empire*. 'But Queen Victoria used to say that she had a vague idea of the state of affairs from her earliest years.'[12]

She was encouraged to be good to please her mother: the Duchess considered exemplary behaviour a requirement of her rank. Unshakeably honest, the young Victoria was candid about her own lapses, describing herself on one occasion in Lehzen's Behaviour Book as 'very very very very horribly naughty!!!!!':[13] evidence does not suggest that as an adult she always continued to acknowledge such shortcomings. In 1884, in his *Celebrated Englishwomen of the Victorian Era*, William Henry Davenport Adams acclaimed Victoria's girlhood as displaying 'a character which all English girls may well do their best to imitate'.[14] It was typical of encomia offered to the ageing monarch. But the truthfulness, frankness and candour of Victoria's younger self, alongside a prematurely earnest avowal of good behaviour, did indeed make her a model of sorts, exactly as her mother intended: in 1831 the Duchess made clear that she wished her child 'to be a pattern of female decorum'.[15] It was a template which, in later years, the inflexible and authoritarian Victoria was apt to modify.

If to modern eyes her education lacked rigour, it was regular and programmatic. Weekly reports were submitted to the Duchess, and every lesson was appraised. By the time of her ninth birthday, the princess's timetable began at eleven in the morning: under the guidance of a number of tutors she worked until four o'clock. A report for the week ending 3 July 1828 shows Victoria studying history, geography, natural history, general knowledge, poetry, religion and orthography with Davys, all, bar 'indifferent' orthography, to a 'good' standard. Mr Westall offered a drawing lesson on Tuesdays, there were writing and arithmetic twice a week, while German and French occupied Victoria for two and three hours a week respectively (French earning an unusual commendation of 'very good' from Monsieur Grandineau). Lessons ended on Thursday with dancing under the instruction of Madame Bourdin.[16]

Victoria's enjoyment was mixed. Throughout her life she was an intellectual pragmatist, mistrusting excessive learning, especially in women, and rightly suspicious that she herself knew less than she ought. She retained a flair for languages and skill in arithmetic. Sketching, drawing and painting were favourite diversions until her sight failed. The Royal Collection owns more than fifty sketchbooks and albums of her watercolours: she sketched whatever pleased her, people and places. 'The dominant quality in the Queen's character,' according to Prince Albert's official biographer Theodore Martin, 'was her strong common-sense.'[17] It is an attribute valued by the British in their constitutional monarchs but one distinct from intellectualism. The lesson Victoria took most to heart was learnt at her mother's, or Lehzen's, knee: the cause-and-effect morality of the children's stories of Maria Edgeworth and evangelical didact Mrs Trimmer, rewards for the good, punishments for the bad, resourcefulness and initiative traits close to godliness. That concept of idealised behaviour, closely related to duty, would remain with Victoria, moulding her intentions if not always her actions: she never successfully separated her sense of herself from that of her position. In preparation for queen-ship, as William IV's health spiralled ever downward, in March 1837, she re-read Edgeworth's stories, steeping herself in their black-and-white world of sowing and reaping. It was an ambiguous preliminary to a life which must necessarily include many shades of grey.

Her education had been shaped by precepts which would become a mania as the century advanced: the importance of 'regulating the passions, securing morality and establishing a sound religion' extolled by Miss Elizabeth Appleton in a manual on early education published in 1821 and dedicated to the Duchess.[18] As it happened, only Albert ever persuaded Victoria to regulate her passionate temper, in lessons that were painful to teacher and pupil. After his death, there would be signs of backsliding.

Occasionally, the results of the Duchess's system were displayed to key individuals. After one encounter with Victoria, Harriet Arbuthnot, discreet but sharp-tongued confidante of the Duke of Wellington, noted, 'The Duchess of Kent is a very sensible person & educates her remarkably well.'[19] If that were the case, Victoria herself was not the only intended beneficiary. Pressed by Conroy, the Duchess meant the world to acknowledge her fitness to direct the future monarch. She cherished a particular ambition: to be appointed Regent in the event that Victoria succeeded to the throne before her eighteenth birthday. In that aim she was successful, after appointing the Duchess of Northumberland Victoria's governess in 1830 and, in the same year, submitting Victoria (and by extension herself) to examination by the bishops of London and Lincoln. On 2 April, two months short of George IV's death, the Archbishop of Canterbury stated that, 'Her Highness's education in regard to cultivation of intellect, improvement of talent, and religious and moral principle is conducted with so much success as to render any alteration of the system undesirable.'[20] It was a measure of the Duchess's astuteness in pursuit of her goal. The Regency Act received royal assent on 23 December, in the first year of William IV's reign. Parliament also voted an increase in the household's income.

In 1831, Victoria's uncle Leopold became King of the Belgians. He left behind a sister with whom his relations had cooled and his Esher estate of Claremont, where Victoria had briefly escaped the mutton and mistrust of 'Conroyal' life at Kensington. He married a French princess, the graceful, heavily ringletted Louise d'Orléans, in an arranged marriage which forced the devoutly Catholic Louise to place worldly duty above the claims of her faith: it was a sacrifice of a sort that would not be demanded of Victoria. Leopold's henceforth epistolary relationship with his niece became explicitly paternal, bypassing Victoria's mother, Leopold himself 'that *dearest* of Uncles, who has always been to me like a father';[21] '"*il mio secondo padre*" or rather "*solo padre*" for he is indeed like my own father, as I have none'.[22] In the same year, by the Duchess's contrivance, Victoria learnt the nature of her royal destiny: Lehzen slipped inside a history book a genealogical table which made clear the princess's closeness to the throne. Her apocryphal-sounding response, 'I will be good', was unqualified and sincere, although it may as easily have referred to her attitude towards her lessons as any future strategy for sovereignty.

As the years passed, and the atmosphere within Kensington Palace increased in bitterness, Leopold's letters set out a dialogue between monarch and monarch-in-waiting. His advice was torrential – generosity to balance his habitual parsimony. He was not without motive: Britain was a powerful ally for an untested new kingdom like Belgium. Leopold's letters embraced everything from foreign policy to diet and deportment. Their influence on Victoria, as he intended, was profound. In the power struggle which poisoned Kensington life, Leopold, like Lehzen, supported his niece against his sister and her cicisbeo. It made sense in the long term.

Leopold understood monarchy as a masquerade, as in time would Victoria's son Edward VII, the sovereign the principal strutting player; his vision of royalty combined charlatanism with something prim and his goal was survival. If Leopold's view was cynical, it was practical too for a milieu which could not ignore the spectre of revolution. Like Victoria's mother, he enjoined model good behaviour. 'Our times, as I have frequently told you, are hard times for Royalty,' he wrote on 18 October 1833. 'Never was there a period, when the existence of *real qualities in persons in high stations has been more imperiously called for*. It seems that in proportion as sovereign power is abridged, the pretensions and expectations of the public are raised.'[23] Also like his sister, Leopold had mastered the rhetoric of 'Victorianism' *before* Victoria's accession. His propensity for pious maxims and emphatic belief in the importance of the appearance of virtue foreshadow the mindset of the coming reign even before the advent of Albert, who has traditionally been viewed as the architect of Victoria's monarchy. That Victoria would prove a sympathetic and receptive listener is shown in her response to Lehzen's disclosure and that unexpected family tree: 'Now – many a child would boast, but they don't know the difficulty; there is much splendour, but there is more responsibility!'[24] For seventy years Victoria would sing from the same song sheet (for a period during the 1860s she overlooked the splendour entirely and defined the responsibility to suit herself). Her refutation of her Hanoverian forebears consisted of that single sentence. No more was needed.

In the meantime the household at Kensington Palace was engaged in a waiting game. In *Coming Events*, the first playlet in his 'dramatic biography' of Queen Victoria, *Happy and Glorious*, Laurence Housman has Victoria read aloud from the Book of Proverbs: 'Hope deferred maketh the heart sick: but when the desire cometh it is a tree of life.'[25] Victoria, the Duchess, Conroy, Lehzen and, in Belgium, Leopold all awaited the coming of the same desire, the death of William IV without issue. So too, Baroness Späth's replacement, Lady of the Bedchamber Lady Flora Hastings, an ill-omened acolyte of Conroy's, commended for her elegant manners and 'vivacity' if not for her ability to combine extreme piety with witticisms of coruscating spite. In several cases, their motives differed. So too the benefits they would separately derive from the new reign.

'Eccentric and singular', given to choleric spluttering and in questionable health, of 'very confined understanding and very defective education',[26] William himself was nevertheless aware of the furious tussles that soured the Duchess's establishment, their origin and intent. Only

Victoria escaped the King's animosity. At Windsor Castle on 21 August 1836, at his seventy-first birthday dinner, William IV stated his determination to outlive his niece's minority: 'I trust to God that my life may be spared for nine months longer, after which period, in the event of my death, no Regency would take place. I should then have the satisfaction of leaving the royal authority to the personal exercise of that Young Lady, the Heiress Presumptive of the Crown, and not in the hands of a person now near me, who is surrounded by evil advisers and who is herself incompetent to act with propriety in the situation in which she would be placed.'[27] A dutiful (if disillusioned) daughter, at her uncle's conniption, Victoria burst into tears.

The King's prayer was answered. He died less than a month after Victoria's eighteenth birthday, on 20 June 1837. The following week Victoria received a letter offering her 'sincerest felicitations on that great change which [has] taken place in your life'. The writer was Albert of Saxe-Coburg and Gotha, a romantic-looking Teuton on the cusp of what proved to be timely physical perfection: long-limbed, delicate in his features, bristling with the gloss of untainted virility. He addressed the new sovereign twice over – as 'Queen of the mightiest land in Europe' and 'dearest cousin' – and, with a mixture of coyness and conniving that would prove invaluable in expediting future relations, ended, 'May I pray you to think . . . sometimes of your cousins in Bonn.'[28]

His prayer too would be answered.

3

'Constant amusements, flattery, excitements and mere politics'

VICTORIA RECEIVED NEWS of her accession in her nightclothes. At six o'clock in the morning, as dawn gilded a sleeping city, the Lord Chamberlain and the Archbishop of Canterbury conveyed their tidings. In what would become for Victorians a favourite set-piece of the Queen's personal mythology, described by Mrs Oliphant as certain to form 'a dazzling point in the narrative of the next Macaulay',[1] Victoria emerged from confinement into shafts of sunlight, no longer Nesbit's 'princess in an enchanted palace', henceforth on penny prints and popular engravings 'the Rose of England', a national symbol, a bloom of hope. Thomas Carlyle observed that she was 'at an age when a girl can hardly be trusted to choose a bonnet for herself'. She was young but not too young, this Sleeping Beauty awoken to new life within weeks of attaining her majority.

The life she inherited was a compound of duty, deskwork and exaltation. As imagined by artist H. T. Wells in 1887, Victoria stands centre stage, bathed in the light of a new day, ethereal in her shimmering whiteness, doe eyes resolute but feeling. The composition suggests earlier images of the Annunciation: the Virgin learning of her choice by God. (In this case, Victoria occupied the place of the angel.) It was not an accident. Over time Victoria's role would incorporate elements matriarchal and quasi-divine. In 1839, she became the first woman on the throne to combine the roles of monarch and mother; in 1897, at her Diamond Jubilee, she attained tabloid apotheosis when the *Daily Mail* extolled her as surpassed in majesty by God alone.

Later on that first morning, Victoria attended a meeting of the Privy Council. She wore black for her uncle's death. In David Wilkie's painting of the scene, black gave way to white. Future Tory premier Sir Robert Peel expressed amazement at 'her manner . . ., at her apparent deep sense of her situation, and at her firmness'.[2] All too soon he would have cause to remember that first impression, as would those throughout her reign who found themselves in opposition to Victoria's will, members of her own family included. Victoria for her part was at pains to deny her nervousness. Looking back in 1886, she claimed, 'The Queen was *not* overwhelmed on her accession – rather full of courage, she may say. *She took things as they came, as she knew they must be.*'[3] Official business aside, she ordered that a bed be made up for her in a room of her own at Kensington Palace. The Duchess rightly interpreted the shift as symbolic. Ditto the new Queen's refusal of her mother's request that Conroy and Lady Flora Hastings attend the Duchess at the proclamation of her accession: it was too soon for clemency. On three occasions at the outset of Victoria's reign, the poet Elizabeth Barrett attempted to imagine her feelings. 'Victoria's Tears' presents one version of the proclamation ceremony. But Barrett underestimated her heroine. The poet's refrain, 'She wept, to wear a crown!'

was not Victoria's. In the latter's journal for the first day of her reign, a single word dominated: *alone*. It was a statement of exultation.

Victoria would continue to regard sovereignty as a lonely business. In the beginning she fought to keep it so – first from her mother and that 'Arch-Fiend', the 'Monster and demon Incarnate', John Conroy, who would never now escape the intense hatred Victoria had conceived for him when he tried to force her to appoint him her private secretary in the autumn of 1835 as she battled typhoid fever; subsequently, in the early years of marriage, from her husband. Later she prevented her eldest son, Bertie, from sharing her burden, apparently untroubled by the piquant contrariness which permitted her to castigate Bertie for futility even as she denied him any alternative.

Earliest commentators focused on Victoria's diminutive height: she was 'the little queen', 'her little majesty'. The adjective suggests infantilisation and, mistakenly, a quality akin to negligibility, neutering the threat of the first female sovereign since the dropsical Queen Anne of chequered record: the subversive re-envisioned as simply small. Physically the new Queen *was* little: most accounts agree on a height of four feet eleven inches. Moreover the Kensington system had deliberately stunted her experience. But her thoughts began to soar even before her accession. 'I do not suppose myself quite equal to all,' she had written to Leopold with fine equivocation during William IV's last illness; 'I trust, however, that with *good-will, honesty,* and *courage,* I shall not at all events, *fail.*'[4] Leopold's response had been to dispatch to London Baron Christian Stockmar, liberal-minded éminence grise of the Coburg dynasty, physician and Leopold's confidential adviser, 'the most discreet man, the most well-judging, and most cool man'; he attended Victoria at breakfast on the morning of her accession and remained on call for the next twenty years.[5] A political polymath of chilly wisdom committed to the spread of constitutional monarchy and, in Leopold's words, 'a *living* dictionary of all matters scientific and political that happened these thirty years',[6] Stockmar too played his part in the evolution of 'Victorian' Victoria. In July, Mary, Duchess of Gloucester, indiscreet, once beautiful tell-tale daughter of George III, wrote to her brother Ernest, 'I really pity the Queen, for she has no soul about her to tell her what she ought to do.' That had never been the case and would not be so until 1861. Thanks to Stockmar, and to Leopold's assiduousness as correspondent, it was not so now. Mary's assertion that, 'I really think that she is disposed to what is right if put in the right way' came closer to the mark.[7] In 1837, Victoria's 'littleness' did not proscribe her good intentions; pettiness came later. Unabashed in her eminence, she vowed in the beginning to exert herself in pursuit of a greater good: 'I shall do my utmost to fulfil my duty towards my country; I am very young and perhaps in many, though not in all things, inexperienced, but I am sure, that very few have more real good will and more real desire to do what is fit and right than I have.'[8] It is a rebuttal of sorts of Carlyle's poxy dismissal.

Through the mid-1830s, as Victoria's accession advanced from possibility to likelihood, the princess had been revealed to her future subjects in a series of stately 'progresses' around England and Wales organised, to the intense irritation of the King, by Conroy and the Duchess of Kent. Engravings of her portraits also circulated. In those images – by Henry Collen and George Hayter – Victoria dressed her hair not in the current style of the day, made fashionable by Queen Adelaide, but like deceased cousin Charlotte, a plaited coronet symbolically on the crown of her head. This iconographic kinship was an expression of continuity and of the younger heiress presumptive's right to rule. With the throne hers, Victoria's thoughts abandoned Charlotte: henceforth the cousins shared only a passion for music and their affection for Leopold. Charlotte had been 'forward, dogmatical on all subjects, buckish about horses, and full of exclamations very like swearing', a perfect compound of her disreputably unprissy parents.[9] Determined to be 'good', Victoria would emulate her cousin only in being 'dogmatical'.

The new Queen described 'the good humour and excessive loyalty' of the large crowds who turned out to witness her lavish but comically under-rehearsed coronation on 28 June 1838 as 'beyond everything, and I really cannot say *how* proud I feel to be the Queen of *such* a *Nation*'.[10] Queen and country were united in mutual admiration, demand for coronation newspapers so high that the Post Office was forced to organise extra carriages to transport them to the provinces.[11] It looked as though the prophecy of Barrett's 'The Young Queen', published in *The Athenaeum* on 1 July 1837, had been fulfilled: 'the grateful isles/ Shall give thee back their smiles'. Throughout that first year, smiles pursued Victoria's progress, friendly crowds 'thronging, bustling, gaping, and gazing at everything, at anything, or at nothing', as Greville recorded; afterwards Victoria described 1837 as 'the pleasantest summer I *EVER* passed in *my life*'. She was acclaimed as 'the Queen of Hearts': 'loved soon as seen'.[12] Flattered, naive and willing to please, Victoria formulated resolutions with dizzying zeal: 'It is to me the *greatest pleasure* to do my duty for my country and my people, and no fatigue, however great, will be burdensome to me if it is for the welfare of the nation.'[13] She did not recognise that the country responded to her youth and her Lilliputian femininity: their reaction was not to her personally.

Instead, in the aftermath of the Reform Act of 1832, with its symbolic extension of the franchise, the numberless watchers glimpsed in her the promise of a new start. 'The accession of our young queen is a circumstance full of hope and promise,' asserted the *Manchester Guardian*. Victoria was the sovereign created in the climate of reform; the newspaper claimed on her behalf sympathy with reformers' aims: 'As the first sovereign who has acceded to the throne since the time of our great political regeneration, her feelings, it seems to us, must be much identified with that important measure, and her principles inclined to the furtherance of those objects which were looked to as its natural results.'[14] In the month of Victoria's accession, an unnamed poetaster in *Blackwood's Edinburgh Magazine* offered: 'With glowing hopes our bosoms burn,/ Our hearts with eager fondness yearn;/ Millions in thee an interest claim –'[15] Victoria herself apparently told Lady Cowper, 'that sometimes when she wakes of a morning she is quite afraid that it should be all a dream'.[16] It was indeed a moment for optimism.

Since 1760, court and government had existed in a virtual stranglehold of Toryism: from the throne George III and his two eldest sons had all supported the Tory party. Imprecisely if unconcernedly political at this stage, Victoria was by upbringing a Whig, warmly sympathetic to that aristocratic party which, opposing the Tories, upheld the supremacy of Parliament over monarchy and advanced, with unsteady conviction, an agenda for reform; the Duke of Kent had favoured intermittent liberal-mindedness, his duchess too. The general election necessitated by Victoria's accession – the last of its sort in British history – returned a Whig government with a small majority. At its head was a man of few political convictions ideally suited to becoming Victoria's mentor.

William Lamb, 2nd Viscount Melbourne, was above all externally insouciant. Wry and charmingly disdainful, he was urbane, patrician and ironical, dilettantish even in his philandering: a cynic along Leopold's lines but without the latter's affectation of rectitude. He struggled to interest himself fully in politics. Averse to dogma, responsible but without the impulse to pontificate, he was persuaded only of the rightness of aristocratic government and the folly of tinkering, a Regency figure whose weary glamour seduced a Victoria unused to men and still happy to be amused. By 1837, more than a decade had passed since the death of Melbourne's impossible and unstable wife, Lady Caroline Lamb; the couple's epileptic only son was also dead. The relationship that Melbourne established so swiftly with his royal mistress, a rapport so absorbing that rumours described them as considering marriage, is testament to personal chemistry, his own astuteness and the neediness of both – in Victoria's case for guidance and a father figure, in Melbourne's for diversion and an emotional outlet. Forty years separated them. Beneath the Queen's veneer of youth was a steeliness born of protracted struggles with Conroy and her mother. It was balanced by a lack of confidence and a degree of immaturity which, as he later confessed to Albert, initially unsettled the older man. Melbourne became for Victoria a tragic-romantic figure whom she sketched over and over again: still handsome with his grey eyes and sonorous voice, bearing with such lightness the imprint of an emotional life that was at the same time rackety and affecting. To modern eyes they appear an unlikely couple to have inspired in editors of a northern newspaper any certainty of civic-mindedness. Their personal honeymoon period, in which 'Lord M' was almost constantly at Victoria's beck and call, shaping her understanding of politics and the government process, was also that of the new reign. It would not last. Not until the decade of jubilees did Victoria regain the giddily unquestioning adulation granted her in the summer of 1837.

For all her good intentions she did not mean to reform her wilfulness. She addressed the problem of her mother with childish heavy-handedness, banishing the Duchess to quarters remote from her own in Buckingham Palace; communication took the form of hastily scribbled notes. 'Neither a particle of affection nor of respect' remained in Victoria's feelings towards her mother, according to the Duke of Wellington.[17] Lehzen by contrast, retained her cherished status as '*precious* Lehzen . . . my "best and truest" friend I have had', and was permitted largely unfettered access to Victoria. If the atmosphere at court was markedly better than that formerly at Kensington Palace, grounds for acrimony between mother and daughter persisted. For her birthday in 1838, the Duchess of Kent presented Victoria with a copy of *King Lear*, Shakespeare's tragedy of ingratitude; Melbourne did nothing to counter Victoria's opinion of the Duchess as a 'liar and a hypocrite'. Victoria was peremptory and obstinate on all occasions, quick to consult her own desires and inclinations: her courtiers' language of deference included few words of caution. On state occasions mother and daughter enacted loving kindness. To the intelligent, or malicious, observer the tensions were palpable. Such an atmosphere partly explains those instances of misguided behaviour – the Flora Hastings Affair and the Bedchamber Crisis – which soon convinced politicians and courtiers alike that the time for Victoria's marriage was approaching.

Even Victoria herself was shortly reconciled to overcoming her 'great reluctance' to change her state.

Five years previously Leopold had written to his niece on the importance of good behaviour: 'By the dispensation of providence you are destined to fill a most eminent station, and to fill it *well*, must now become your study. A good heart and a truly honourable character are amongst the most indispensable qualifications for that position.'[18] The young Victoria came close to ignoring both.

Pride and prejudice more than honour or a good heart shaped the Queen's conduct in the Flora Hastings Affair and the Bedchamber Crisis. Both debacles tarnished Victoria's reputation and spoilt her early pleasure in her queenship. In government circles they emphasised the dangers of any overlap of the personal and the political in the court life of a young and inexperienced sovereign, and undermined Victoria's perceived fitness to exercise her remaining constitutional powers.

Flora Hastings, daughter of a Tory grandee, was an appointment of Sir John Conroy's to the household of the Duchess of Kent. Her sympathies lay with her employer and her sponsor. Willowy in her spinsterhood, religious too, she nevertheless possessed a forked tongue: frequently in her conversation malice and wit merged. To Victoria, who lacked confidence in her own intellectual abilities, it was an unappealing trait exacerbated by her suspicion that Lady Flora spied on her. This wholly negative assessment is what made possible her treatment of the hapless lady-in-waiting in a manner that was both cruel and deadly in its flippancy.

Lady Flora's misfortune consisted of a coincidence and medical bungling. On her return from Scotland to London in the New Year of 1839, she shared a post-chaise with

Conroy. Innocent it may have been: it was certainly unwise not to conceal so incendiary an indiscretion. That journey, however, cannot have inspired the tumour of the liver which, on 5 July, killed her.

Within days of Lady Flora's return, Victoria's court interpreted her swollen abdomen as evidence of pregnancy. Apprised of her journey with Conroy, assumptions were made – including by Victoria – and afterwards confirmed by inept royal doctor Sir James Clark, who did not trouble himself to examine the patient. Speculation mounted. To maintain the new court's reputation for moral probity, Lady Flora was forced to submit to a full examination, which found her without child and still a virgin. It ought to have been an end to the matter.

But Victoria's hatred for Conroy admitted no moderation. By neither word nor action did she move to clear Lady Flora's name. Clark himself further muddied the waters with his startling suggestion that the appearance of virginity did not preclude pregnancy. Melbourne too was sceptical. No surprise that the Hastings family became incensed and, against advice, made their grievances public. Once the witch-hunt was exposed in the pages of *The Times*, there was little credit for Victoria in belatedly granting to Lady Flora that audience in which monarch and dying woman embraced and agreed to a truce for the sake of the Duchess. Neither the Hastings family nor the public was mollified. Reluctantly Victoria agreed to a further meeting. Days away from death, prostrate and skeletal bar her grotesquely swollen stomach, the wronged spinster clasped Victoria's hand. Even so pitiful a sight, which forced Victoria's compassion, did not move her to apologise. Rather the proximity of this '*nasty* woman' dying under her own roof troubled and indeed irked her.

Small consolation for Lady Flora that she died 'the victim of a depraved court', her own the heroine's part.

While the press disgorged this unedifying hullabaloo from which neither Victoria nor Melbourne emerged with credit, the Prime Minister was wrestling with problems of a different variety. Within Parliament his government faced defeat. For Victoria the prospect of losing Lord M was not one she could regard with equanimity. Her very strong feelings on the matter had little to do with politics or the good of the country. It was her own convenience, her own happiness, her own benefit that she considered. 'The simple truth,' according to Greville, '[was] that the Queen could not endure the thought of parting with Melbourne who [was] everything to her.'[19] Melbourne's resignation, on 7 May 1839, plunged her into despair: she cried, she panicked, she felt it like a physical blow. Unsettled if unrepentant as the scandal surrounding Lady Flora ground relentlessly on, she *needed* Lord M.

Or did she? If Victoria wanted allies against the Hastings family, surrounded as she was by courtiers and companions, she did not have far to look. Her formal entourage consisted of her mistress of the robes, eight ladies of the bedchamber, eight women of the bedchamber and eight maids of honour, a substantial support network given the women's overwhelmingly Whig sympathies. With Lord M at her side they constituted Victoria's second line of defence. Without him, they became an essential bulwark between Victoria and her conscience.

While the Whigs floundered, Sir Robert Peel was called upon to form a government. Oxford-educated son of a textiles manufacturer, tall but diffident, sporadically gauche, limp-haired but stiff in his manner, Peel correctly doubted Victoria's sympathy. He required a token endorsement of his ministry: some Tory ladies among the royal attendants. It was a tinderbox request. Victoria would not yield. If she could not have Lord M, she would not be surrounded by Peel's creatures crowing her defeat, not even one of them. She determined to stand her ground. Had not King Leopold once told her, 'as a fundamental rule . . . be courageous, firm and honest'? Melbourne himself had echoed that advice: she must overcome personal inclination, treat the new ministry with fairness and a show of amiability – and make it clear that she hoped her household would not be subject to a cull. So recently Peel had observed Victoria's firmness and her conviction of her own position. He could match her intransigence. Politely, fixedly, sovereign and minister engaged in a contest for mastery, a loveless *pas de deux*. Victoria continued to take advice from Melbourne, although he flouted constitutional propriety with every word he wrote to her, lessening with every instance of her persisting dependency her chances of political impartiality. Inevitably his advice strengthened her resolve. She refused to surrender a single lady.

Once before, a man of slipshod manners whom she disliked had tried to force Victoria's hand. She had not yielded to Sir John Conroy and she would not give way to Sir Robert Peel. She observed his discomfort in her presence, bolstered by Melbourne's disdainful verdict that Sir Robert, though 'a very gifted and able man', was 'an underbred fellow . . . not accustomed to talk to Kings and Princes'.[20] Undoubtedly the anguish of the Flora Hastings Affair influenced Victoria's judgement. In her response to Peel's request were suggestions of amateur dramatics run riot: 'I was calm but very decided,' she wrote to Melbourne of the critical interview. 'I think you would have been pleased to see my composure and great firmness. The

Queen of England will not submit to such trickery.'[21] The soldier's daughter had tasted the scent of blood: she embraced the rhetoric of triumphalism. This vigorous note would return – in her Boudicca-like response to the Crimean and Boer Wars and her imperturbability in the face of eight assassination attempts. Less attractively it coloured her personal relationships too: with her children and with other prime ministers she could not like, Palmerston and Gladstone. 'They wished to treat me like a girl,' Victoria told Lord M, 'but I will show them that I am Queen of England.' Such airy bluster was an inevitable legacy of the Duchess's and Conroy's mistreatment of the young Victoria; for the rest of her life she blotted out girlish vulnerability by asserting her impregnability as Queen of England.

In May 1839, her differences with Peel became truly a battle royal: Victoria's part, had she but known it, anticipated the empty bravado of Lewis Carroll's Red Queen – rank without reason. Her refusal to compromise was met by a similar refusal on Peel's part, who declined to form a government on Victoria's terms. The Whigs returned to power by default. Victoria once again had her Lord M. That night, buoyant with victory, she danced until quarter past three in the morning in the company of Tsarevitch Alexander of Russia, uncomprehending both of the battle she had fought and the significance of its outcome. In her exhilaration she even imagined herself '(talking jokingly) . . . a little in love' with her distinguished foreign guest: he was 'a dear, delightful young man'.

In March 1851, Victoria's new poet laureate Alfred Tennyson celebrated the 'Victorian' virtues of the Queen's court:

> Her court was pure; her life serene;
> God gave her peace; her land reposed
> A thousand claims to reverence closed
> In her . . .[22]

What came near to truthfulness in 1851 was mere flattery in 1839. It was marriage which made good the transition and endowed Victoria with the possibility both of serenity and peace. From her vantage point as a widow, recalling that marriage of notable happiness, Victoria reappraised the early, unmarried years of her reign. Writing of herself in the third person, she told biographer Theodore Martin that the period 1837 to 1840 'was the least sensible and satisfactory time in her whole life . . . That life of constant amusement, flattery, excitements and mere politics had a bad effect (as it must have upon any one) on her naturally simple and serious nature.'[23] Like much self-assessment, it contained elements of truth: there *was* a simplicity to Victoria's nature, she was candid, honest and occasionally unforgiving in her self-appraisal. But those bulging Hanoverian eyes were not all-seeing and hers was not a nature that inclined easily to selflessness. As we shall see, Victoria would achieve detachment at a cost.

4

'Every quality that could be desired to render me perfectly happy'

THE NINETEEN-YEAR-OLD VICTORIA regards the viewer with a combination of calculation and hesitancy in her portrait by William Fowler, a middling practitioner, for which she sat on 10 August 1838: crowned with a diadem, snowy shoulders wrapped in folds of ermine, Garter-starred, erect in her bearing, her lips character-istically parted. According to the *Court Circular*, the portrait received a royal viewing on 14 August 1840, when it was shown to King Leopold at Claremont. His verdict was positive.[1]

Leopold, that cautious Svengali, had reason for appro-bation. In the two years since Fowler's sitting, Victoria's uncle had brought to fruition a scheme very close to his heart. If Fowler's image – at least the third he had painted of Victoria since 1825 – suggests anticipation and expec-tancy, its promise had been fulfilled by the time of its unveiling. An engraving of the portrait, undertaken by B. P. Gibbon, had already been published on 10 February. It was the day of Victoria's wedding.

Like her uncle George IV, Victoria married her first cousin. Unlike that earlier marriage, Victoria's was to be one of surpassing devotion, full, she claimed, 'of the friendship, kindness and affection which a truly happy marriage brings with it'.[2] Her choice was limited; it was an eventuality for which she had been prepared in advance. Leopold lay behind it, as in her father's marriage. As in her father's marriage, Leopold chose as spouse a member of his own family.

'Uncle's great wish – was – that I should marry my Cousin, Albert,' Victoria told Melbourne on 18 April 1839,[3] in a conversation broached, after some prevarication, with the aim of postponing just that 'schocking alternative' to her single state (the description – and the spelling – are her own). Albert was the younger son of Leopold's reprobate eldest brother Ernest, a man of easygoing loucheness who, since 1826, had ruled over the newly united duchies of Saxe-Coburg and Gotha. These insignificant territories in Thuringia and Saxony had a population twice that of the Isle of Wight, but granted their duke an assumption of *droit du seigneur* which he exploited with vigour; even in his portrait by the fatuously benign Sir George Hayter, he betrays a shifty opportunism. As if to suggest a theme, Albert's mother had been banished for adultery when Albert was five. He was twelve at the time of her death from cancer, with a passion for forming orderly collections, a dreamy engagement with the countryside of his homeland, a deep attachment to his flawed and fissured family and, as he frequently complained, a weak stomach. This combination of idealism, administrative efficiency and lack of physical robustness would persist. He was a curious product of so thrustingly sexy and gossip-riddled a provincial court. The sensitive child of an insensitive and boisterous father and a tragic if fallible mother, a poor relation whose intellectual life was richer than that of the woman he married, his contemplative life both more resourceful and more deliberate, like Leopold before him Albert would be welcomed warmly by his new wife and coldly by his adopted country. By inclination he was an outsider: friendlessness would form an aspect of his life in England.

For a time Victoria herself had permitted her emotions to fluctuate. It was neither dilatoriness nor callousness which held her back; nor was she heedless of Leopold's plan – she had been party to the latter's supervision of the final stages of Albert's education. Rather she baulked at her own accurate assessment that her obstinate and intractable nature was ill suited to the submissiveness which she recognised as part of marriage. (At the age of thirteen she had been so forcefully impressed by Katherina's speech of surrender to her husband Petruchio at the end of a performance of *The Taming of the Shrew* that she sketched the scene from memory.[4]) After their first meeting, in June 1836, Victoria admitted to Leopold the good impressions she had formed of Albert: 'I must thank you, my beloved Uncle, for the prospect of great happiness, you have contributed to give me, in the person of dear Albert. Allow me, then, my dearest Uncle, to tell you how delighted I am with him, and how much I like him in every way. He possesses every quality that could be desired to render me perfectly happy. He is so sensible, so kind, and so good, and so amiable too. He has besides, the most pleasing and delightful exterior and appearance, you can possibly see.'[5] From the vexed fastness of Kensington Palace, the seventeen-year-old princess, stifled by her mother, found in her uncle a welcome ally and, in his plans for her, release from her confinement. Three years later, the prospect of such an escape was regarded with less relish by a headstrong Queen of England at the centre of a silly, if spirited, court which could be set rocking with laughter, for example, by the tomfoolery of the Lord Chamberlain's sons when waltzing. Anticipating a second visit by Albert, Victoria was at pains to deny that she had made either him, or Leopold, any sort of promise. Decidedly she would not commit herself to marriage in a hurry: 'at the *very earliest*, any such event could not take place till *two or three years hence*'.

This miss-ish self-importance and arbitrary schedule of avoidance were soon overcome. In Victoria's eyes, the intervening three years had 'embellished' Albert's 'pleasing and delightful' exterior to devastating effect. His hair had grown darker, though something of his resemblance to the elfin, vanished mother remained, distinguishing him from his swarthier, heartier-looking brother with whom he travelled. His shoulders were broader; breathlessly Victoria noticed the shapeliness of his limbs in white cazimere pantaloons with '*nothing under them*'; his waist was narrow (waistlines were much on Victoria's mind: for the first time she was wrestling unsuccessfully with her own expanding girth). It was the same verdict which Lady Granville confessed that she, Lady Sandwich and Lady Clanricarde had all reached;[6] so, too, Melbourne's sister Lady Cowper, who noted 'a good figure and well built'.[7] On 10 October 1839, before any such observations could be put into words, Victoria fell in love. It was a *coup de foudre* – instantaneous – and it washed over her unannounced and unanticipated as she waited at the top of a staircase at Windsor Castle for her cousins' arrival and beheld the seraphic vision. Hanoverian effusiveness and a keenly physical excitement demolished all her prosy resolve. Despite her best intentions she was ever impulsive and hot-blooded.

To herself she did not trouble to dissemble. She confided to her journal, 'It was with some emotion that I beheld

Albert – who is *beautiful*.' In that spirit of fairness which was among her most appealing qualities, she wrote to Leopold to reassure him and to recant her earlier objections. Five days later, having confirmed her extraordinary feelings in her own mind, Victoria proposed to her cousin. 'Ordinarily it is not what a woman would wish to say herself. She would rather – *he* said it,' Laurence Housman's Victoria tells Albert in *Woman Proposes*.[8] Royal etiquette forbade an alternative. It was an undertaking sufficiently quaint to inspire cartoons and lithographs when the news was made public. To her aunt Mary, Duchess of Gloucester, Victoria acknowledged that the experience of playing the man's part had been an awkward one. It was not a sensation on which she had previously much reflected and yet it applied to so many aspects of her position as queen regnant. Following her marriage to Albert, she would brood on it frequently. Beneath that 'beautiful' exterior, Albert was set on mastery.

In the nation at large, Victoria's choice was not a popular one: in that respect Melbourne had found it impossible to advise her accurately, voicing by turns the Coburgs' adverse reputation for go-getting and Albert's own recommendations. That this should be so was also partly attributable to Leopold. For the ambitious King of the Belgians, himself once a threadbare prince of Saxe-Coburg, continued to meet his English expenses, including the upkeep of his estate at Claremont, from the generous pension provided him by Parliament as the widower of Princess Charlotte. Such evident self-serving outraged Parliament and influenced its grant to Albert of an annuity of £30,000 against the customary £50,000 which Leopold had been voted. Uselessly Victoria seethed. Her anger was divided between the Tories, whom she suspected of scoring points off Lord Melbourne and paying her back for her part in the Bedchamber Crisis

– both at Albert's expense; and her own helplessness: no matter how often she invoked the precedent of Queen Anne's 'very stupid and insignificant' husband, George of Denmark, she could not empower Melbourne to wave a magic wand. Cartoons and doggerel cheerfully labelled Albert a fortune-hunter: 'He comes to take "for better or worse"/ England's fat Queen and England's fatter purse.'[9] Victoria's proposal inspired many emotions in Albert, who had yet to fall in love with his cousin: pleasure in his material good fortune does not appear to have been uppermost. In the four months which elapsed before his wedding, continuous setbacks and petty humiliations – over his title, his rank and precedence, and the composition of his household, whose members he would not be allowed to nominate for himself – did much in Albert's own mind to counter the argument that it was he who benefited from the alliance. 'As to your wish about your gentlemen, my dear Albert,' Victoria wrote in response to his request that he choose his own private secretary in place of Melbourne's cast-off, George Anson, 'I must tell you quite honestly that it will not do.' He would retain the services of Isaac Cart, the valet he had shared with his brother Ernest; his only other souvenir of home was his greyhound Eos. Little wonder Albert confided to a boyhood friend that his future, though 'brilliant', was 'plentifully strewn with thorns'.

Inequalities in their relationship notwithstanding, what both cousins gained was an assurance of companionship. Granted, Victoria had put behind her on her accession the loneliness of her secluded childhood: at the centre of her pleasure-loving court, she was seldom alone. Yet she lacked fulfilling relationships and had few close friends among the aristocracy whose members made up her attendants and ministers. While she clung to the warm familiarity of Lehzen and Melbourne, her heart was ripe for plucking:

she needed the company of those of her own age. Her sketchbooks prove her susceptibility to a handsome face: a Count Waldstein distantly related to the Duchess of Kent, the glamorous exile Charles, Duke of Brunswick and his companion Count d'Anglau, and the Tsarevitch Alexander all had her pulse and her pencil racing.[10] All were men with whom Victoria's engagement was overwhelmingly imaginative, shaped by her cultural, rather than her emotional, exposure: she did not even meet Brunswick, her second cousin, but glimpsed him, dark and artfully dishevelled, across a crowded theatre and riding in the park. And in her imagination, these identikit young men had more in common with the heroes of the Italian opera or contemporary fiction than the flesh and blood offshoots of the *Almanach de Gotha*. With his combination of physical perfection and sensitivity, his love of art, music and history, his skill at fencing and skating and his bravery on the hunting field, and those intimations of physical ardour of a different sort which she discerned in his kisses and fond endearments, Albert embodied all the cravings Victoria had transposed upon these two-dimensional lotharios. In addition, like Victoria, he was steeped in the fiction of Sir Walter Scott, which his step-grandmother, the Dowager Duchess of Saxe-Gotha-Altenburg, had read to him as a child: its rosy and hot-blooded historicism, embraced by husband and wife, inspired the fantasy that became Balmoral, a glittering granite castle far from London, like Ellen's Isle in *The Lady of the Lake* a place where courtly formalities gave way to a simpler idyll.[11] The landscape of Victoria and Albert's childhoods differed physically and emotionally: the imaginative perimeters of their formative years overlapped in significant ways.

In the aftermath of her proposal, Victoria commissioned Albert's portrait from miniaturist William Ross. On 29

October she described herself as 'very anxious' about it, presumably on account of her habitual impatience and her pressing desire that Ross, who, she told Melbourne liked to make his sitters look worse rather than better than their everyday selves,[12] do justice to his subject.[13] To that near impossible challenge, the artist apparently rose. On 7 January 1840, Victoria recorded delivery of the finished image: '[it] is now and always standing before me. It is quite speaking and is my delight.'[14]

Ownership of Albert's image, created in accordance with her own instructions, was a form of emotional possession, measure of the force of Victoria's love and the nature of her emotional need; the language the image spoke was that ascribed to it by Victoria. On so many different levels Albert was her subject. Like those pristine wooden dolls dressed and catalogued in Lehzen's company, Ross's Albert – the first of myriad representations of this paragon among princes – was endowed by Victoria with attributes of her own devising and her own requirement.

For Victoria Albert was an 'Angel': the label adhered during those first perfervid weeks of their engagement never to be discarded. Repeatedly she hailed him as her superior in almost every way. And yet, although she acted unconsciously, she was powerless to resist the urge to cut her 'Angel' down to size and refashion him according to her own lights – the heavenly being whose portrait in miniature she wore in a bracelet. For Victoria the Queen, stubborn, hot-blooded and autocratic, this painted Albert became a talisman of love, a trinket caught in a jewelled embrace firmly within her own control. She was apparently unaware that she had blundered into a contradiction. Albert, by contrast, devoted the weeks the couple spent together following their betrothal to indulging Victoria. Only afterwards did he sedulously embark on the process of forging his own improved 'Albertine' Victoria. That process, which he undertook with rigour in the early years of marriage, consisted of breaking and remoulding his wife's character in pursuit of an ideal of the rational, sensible, unselfish public servant partly shaped by Leopold and Stockmar. Unlike Victoria's unwitting appropriation of a romanticised, fictionalised Albert, this process was deliberate.

The wedding took place in the Chapel Royal, St James's Palace, after a morning of persistent rain, which only belatedly gave way to sunshine. Guests noted the surprising combination of Victoria's remarkably firm answers and the trembling of her orange blossom headdress; Victoria herself, from the evidence of her journal, noted everything. The service was followed by the briefest of honeymoons, Victoria having reminded Albert that she was 'the Sovereign and that business can stop and wait for nothing'. It was a prim assertion, which expressed strikingly her inability to reconcile the public and private spheres of her fragmented and multiple existence. The implications were not lost on Albert, who ought not to have been surprised.

On 15 November 1837, Victoria had made the first visit of her reign to Drury Lane Theatre. Her subsequent account outlines the nature of the challenge Albert faced. 'I alone was seated in the box which was quite *on* the stage . . . The house was immensely full, quite crammed, and I was *splendidly* received, with the greatest enthusiasm and deafening cheering. When God Save the King was sung, the whole audience joined in the Chorus.' No one, not even Victoria, appeared to notice that the National Anthem had not been emended to suit the new reign.[15] It scarcely mattered. As the embodiment of national spirit and focus of national pride, the sovereign embraced a degree of sexlessness. To the full house at Drury Lane that night, 'Queen' Victoria was also

'King': it was the lustiness of the singing that counted. But it boded badly for Albert, who received no public role on marriage or any unofficial function behind closed doors. Victoria saw her ministers alone and entrusted supervision of her personal expenses to Lehzen, whom Albert would shortly come to loathe. His own purpose was purely repro-ductive, idleness his apportioned lot outside the bedroom – as *Punch* depicted him in 1843 in a sketch entitled 'Cupid Out of Place', in which he appears physically sated but otherwise listless.[16] It was a stark and unwelcome revelation to this passionate auto-didact who, at the age of eleven, had recorded his intention 'to train myself to become a good and useful man'.[17]

Leopold endeavoured to broker a solution. During the same visit on which he viewed Victoria's portrait by Fowler, he expressed his belief that Albert 'ought in business as in everything to be necessary to the Queen, he should be to her a walking dictionary for reference on any point which her own knowledge or education have not enabled her to answer'.[18] Victoria had delighted in Albert helping her with the blotting paper when she signed papers, regarding his assistance as a parry in their extended loveplay, almost a physical intimacy: this shadowy imprint of officialdom was as much as she intended to share with him. Such a stricture was none of Melbourne's doing. The elderly statesman who continued to enjoy Victoria's confidence and her affection – albeit this wistfully worldly man recognised the signs of her coming withdrawal – saw clearly Victoria's deficiencies. To his former private secretary, now Albert's assistant, he wrote, 'I told Her Majesty . . . that there was no objection to her conversing with the Prince on any subject she pleased. My impression is that the chief obstacle in Her Majesty's mind is the fear of difference of opinion and she thinks that domestic harmony is more likely to follow from avoiding subjects likely to create difference.'[19] Victoria was resolute in her determination to have her own way: she did not pause to consider that it was precisely by attempting to avoid differences that she threatened domestic harmony. 'I am only the husband,' Albert complained, 'and not the master of the house.' If the statement included a note of lament, it did not amount to resignation: their arguments would be frequent and fierce.

Albert could not conquer the queen who was also a king, but he could and did conquer the woman. Within months of her wedding, Victoria had discovered that she was pregnant, the very outcome she had dreaded. 'I have always hated the idea,' she wrote. She referred to it as *'die Schattenseite'*, 'the shadow-side of marriage', as if the linguistic shift from English into German pushed it away more firmly. Her emotions were curiously unmixed, fury uppermost, a sense of her own powerlessness hot on its heels. She took pleasure at any rate in Albert's nomination as Regent in June 1840 in the event that childbirth killed her, acquired for him a key to the red boxes of Cabinet papers, but offered no further indications at that point of any transference of power, nominal or otherwise. That would happen in time without Victoria's premeditation. It arose through nine pregnancies and the inevitable withdrawal from the daily business of monarchy which those eighteen years of childbearing enforced.

'He is *perfection*; perfection in every way – in beauty – in everything!' Victoria had written the night of her proposal. 'I told him I was quite unworthy of him . . . I really felt it was the happiest brightest moment of my life, which made up for all I had suffered and endured. Oh! *how* I adore and love him, I cannot say!!'

In time her feelings towards her husband would expand and embrace new spheres of devotion: materially they did not change. Albert remained perfect, Victoria unworthy of him. Loyal in her discipleship to the stories of Edgeworth and Trimmer, she labelled him her reward for the unhappy Kensington years which had not corrupted her. Though she felt herself inadequate to the task, she would apply much of the remainder of her life to enumerating the ways and the extent of her adoration and her love.

As the year drew to a close, Victoria buried a token of her past, with the death of her spaniel Dash. The dog's tombstone claimed that 'his attachment was without selfishness'. Although Victoria cannot have intended it, that simple laudation represented a challenge for both husband and wife.

5

'The cares of Royalty pressed comparatively lightly'

IN THE 1840s the Irish starved. In rural Scotland, the country's poorest grappled with the continuing misery of the Highland Clearances. In England and Wales, in coal-black industrial heartlands, the new urban working classes existed in conditions frequently of abject want: that Stygian cauldron imagined separately by William Blake and Gustave Doré. Unemployment had risen since 1837. Discontent and sporadic rioting greeted the enforcement of the Poor Law Amendment Act of 1834. The solidarity of working men was on the increase. They banded together in pursuit of further constitutional reform: their economic needs keen and biting, their anger targeted their exclusion from the Parliamentary process and government by those untouched by their plight. The movement was called Chartism. Across Europe, similar grievances fomented. In 1848, in Continental capitals large and small, revolution erupted with explosive fury, toppling thrones and princes. 'Old things are falling,' Stockmar wrote, 'times are changing and a new life will come from the ruins.'[1] Not in England. On Kennington

Common in April 1848, Chartism proved a damp squib: 100,000 Special Constables swamped the peaceful meeting.

It was a decade of growing divisions. Novelists, including a future Conservative prime minister of 'very flowery' language, highlighted two nations: in Disraeli's *Sybil*, they were identified as 'the rich and the poor', 'as ignorant of each other's habits, thoughts and feelings as if they were . . . inhabitants of different planets'. Artists reconstructed in appropriately tertiary shades the wretchedness of those for whom industrialisation brought no benefits. Ironically, in the hands of Frank Holl, Luke Fildes and Hubert von Herkomer, such scenes later commanded large sums. The poet Tennyson, not yet called to heel by any appointment to the laureateship, expressed restlessness with the old order: 'A simple maiden in her flower/ Is worth a hundred coats-of-arms.'

Against this backdrop of grit and upheaval, Victoria and Albert evolved a holiday world of escape. It was the first decade of their private neverlands, fantastical houses shaped by childhood memories and paper sketches and airy dreams and snippets of novels and operas: the new Edens of Osborne and Balmoral, acquired respectively in 1845 and 1847. There was nothing furtive in their royal retreat. On the contrary, the couple publicised what were in effect carefully considered stage sets for a new performance monarchy.

In the Hungry Forties, Victoria gave birth to six of her nine children, beginning with Victoria, Princess Royal in 1840. The Prince of Wales, known in the family as Bertie, followed in 1841, then came Alice (1843), Alfred (1844), Helena (1846) and Louise (1848). Arthur, Leopold and Beatrice completed the family: the last was born in 1857, weeks short of Victoria's thirty-eighth birthday.

In addition to nine children, Victoria and Albert bought and built two new royal residences and oversaw extensive alterations to Buckingham Palace, which Victoria described in 1845 as providing a 'total want of accommodation for our growing little family'.[2] Later Albert triumphed in the Great Exhibition of 1851. In 1857, her resistance to sharing her public life long forgotten, Victoria issued Letters Patent investing him with the title Prince Consort; belatedly she endowed him with the status she had continually sought for him – 'Oh! if only I could make him King!' she had yearned in 1845. For throughout this fertile period, despite her emphatic dislike of pregnancy, repeated instances of postnatal depression and her variable attachment to her 'frog-like' children in their earliest infancy, Victoria rejoiced in her increasing harmony and compatibility with her husband; first tensions evaporated. Her own enforced capitulation to domesticity and childbirth was rewarded by Albert's steady encroachment upon her official life, a shift in the sexual politics of their marriage in line with current thinking – as Landseer depicted her in *Queen Victoria and Prince Albert at the Bal Costumé of 12 May 1842*, a diminutive figure swamped by the robes of office, leaning on the firm arm of her husband who so evidently guided her. As time passed, she responded to this development with something like relief. Although her acceptance of women's subjection was wholehearted, she was aware of the unequal weighting of the bargain. 'There is great happiness and great blessedness in devoting oneself to another who is worthy of one's affection,' she wrote later; 'still men are very selfish and the woman's devotion is always one of submission which makes our poor sex so very unenviable.'[3]

'Albert grows daily fonder and fonder of politics and business, and is so wonderfully *fit* for both – such perspicacity and such *courage*,' Victoria wrote to Leopold on 3 February 1852, 'and I grow daily to dislike them both more and more. We women are not *made* for governing – and if we are good women, we must *dislike* these masculine occupations.'[4] It was the very mindset which had enabled Sir John Conroy to attain such ascendancy over the Duchess of Kent, and perhaps implicit in Victoria's first attentiveness to Leopold and her subsequent willing reliance upon Melbourne. Impossible not to regret the bravado of that crowing Queen of England who had so recently refused to be treated like a girl. 'While [Albert] lived,' Theodore Martin intoned, 'the cares of Royalty pressed comparatively lightly upon the Queen.'[5] By the end of the decade she had become in the fullest sense Albert's wife, a process of diminishment by which Victoria became 'Victorian', reborn in the crucible of Albert's limitations. Henceforth she fulfilled a series of contemporary gender stereotypes, which sought to rob her both of vigour and aptitude and to channel her energy towards safely 'female' outlets. She fell casualty to a widely held belief in the sexes' separate spheres, as expounded by Ruskin in 1864: 'Each [sex] has what the other has not: each completes the other, and is completed by the other: they are in nothing alike.'[6] In practice it was a philosophy which denied the possibility of female independence. 'Some day . . . she will become a mother – of *your* children,' Housman has Stockmar tell Albert. 'Then, my Prince, if she still loves you, you will not be her Puppet, nor her Plaything anymore. You will be *King*.'[7] This may indeed have been the blueprint shared by Leopold, Stockmar and Albert, the end to which both older men had clung in directing Albert's studies; it was only partly shaped by cynicism.

Such role reversal demanded Victoria's submergence

of herself in Albert. Serendipitously she contrived to combine self-denial with assertiveness: in adapting herself to Albert's pattern she lost none of her self-identity as Queen of England, even as she helped create in him an ersatz fellow sovereign. The result was the evolution of what historians label the 'dual monarchy'. As he described himself to the Duke of Wellington, Albert had become 'superintendent of [the Queen's] household, manager of her private affairs, her sole confidential adviser in politics, and only assistant in her communications with the officers of the Government, her private secretary, and permanent Minister', a voracious and all-encompassing remit for indispensability, which seems to leave little room for Victoria herself.[8] Yoked together in gilded harness, Victoria and Albert henceforth shared the activities of sovereignty, as closely intertwined as the 'V&A' monogram which became their favourite decorative flourish. A former Cabinet minister dismissed the changed and chastened Victoria as 'Queen Albertine'. 'The Prince is become so identified with the Queen,' wrote Charles Greville in December 1845, 'that they are one person.'[9]

Yet the dualism of their dual monarchy amounted to more than a division of labour, Victoria assuming Albert's reproductive function, Albert filching Victoria's bureaucratic role. It was one of aspect. From 1840 to 1861, Victoria and Albert expanded the cardboard-cutout version of royalty which past monarchs had offered to their subjects: public personae shaped by images of power and wealth. They promoted a vision of their private lives – themselves, their children, their homes, their animals – which celebrated what was ordinary and typical in them, a 'first among equals' variant of royalty which excluded the trappings of rank in order to emphasise the human face of loftiness. As subsequent publication of extracts from Victoria's Highland journals demonstrated, their audience was avid and hungry and responded to this apparent downsizing with increased loyalty and affection. 'They say no Sovereign was ever more loved than I am (I am bold enough to say),' Victoria wrote in 1844, '& this because of our domestic home, the good example it presents.'[10] It was a cult of togetherness and, in an era of increasing moral restrictiveness, suggested blameless royal downtime. Although Victoria may not have acknowledged it, it was 'pattern' behaviour of the sort the Duchess of Kent had enjoined two decades earlier when she urged her daughter to be 'free from all the faults of former reigns'.[11] A lithograph of 1843, *To the Queen's Private Apartments*, depicted Victoria and Albert with their three eldest children. While Victoria dandles Alice on Albert's back, Albert, on all fours, is pulled in different directions by his son, who tugs his necktie, and his eldest daughter, who has harnessed him with a garland of flowers. The father's response is one of happy forbearance. Unobjectionable and endearing, such images suggested a life decorative in its decorousness and delighted their first viewers with glimpses into a formerly hidden world, hidden no longer; a world intended to resemble an idealised version of the viewer's own. It was conduct, as the *Leeds Mercury* had earlier commented, 'such as might have characterised the most loving couple in the middle class of society'.[12]

At the same time, Victoria and Albert kept faith with age-old ceremonial aspects of monarchy. In 1845, Victoria importuned Sir Robert Peel for funds for 'a room [at Buckingham Palace], capable of containing a large number of those persons whom the Queen has to invite in the course of the season to balls, concerts, etc. . . .'[13] The dual rulers transmitted their messages visually, through architecture, portraiture, artistic patronage and even jewellery: brooches and earrings set with the milk teeth of their children, each one a public token of happy consanguinity. Landseer's *Windsor Castle in Modern Times*, begun in 1840, reimagined the ancient citadel of royal power as a framing device for a couple lustrous in their vitality, complete with offspring, dogs and the sfumato effect of young love. But Victoria had no intention of denying her status as queen. She commissioned portraits of herself that asserted and reasserted her majesty. Two portraits of 1843, the year of Alice's birth and Alfred's conception, reference only her role as sovereign. On his second visit to England, Franz Xaver Winterhalter depicted Victoria in the robes of the Order of the Garter in an idiom of uncompromising grandeur, close to hand the Imperial State Crown and the sceptre, her tiny head and shoulders overwhelmed by heavy-duty diamonds; Victoria subsequently described it as 'the portrait she liked best'. Sir Francis Grant, a Scottish painter whose 'sense of beauty derived from the best source, that of really good society',[14] unsurprisingly chose to seat Victoria on a throne; his backdrop is one of similar architectural magnificence and an excess of molten velvet. In both paintings, Victoria wears a diamond diadem fashioned around the emblems of the four kingdoms. It had been commissioned by the most splendid of her uncles, the vain and prickly George IV.

And there was more. The dual monarchy became uniquely a creation of its time, as successfully aligned to contemporary tastes as those shrieking aniline dyes responsible for the heliotrope-coloured fabrics Victoria wore, or the interest in vanished rusticity which made George Eliot's *Adam Bede* a runaway success in 1859: Victoria and Albert commissioned paintings of scenes from the novel and Albert quoted the maxims of its Mrs Poyser. Husband and wife celebrated current preoccupations like family in a manner newly made possible by evolving technology. In March 1842, Albert was first photographed. William Constable had the honour, at his studio in Brighton. Victoria's response, as preserved in her journal for 7 March, was muted: 'Saw the photographs, which are quite good.'[15] Yet two years later, she too sat for the camera. She was not alone. With her was her eldest daughter, Victoria's part not that of queen but mother, and she wore a day dress in place of the ubiquitous diadem, heavily ruffled but not exaggeratedly flattering – like the image itself. Consigning herself to eternal castigation for her lack of amusement, she omitted to smile, her faraway expression part dreamy, part bilious, as if the pressures of her office were indeed inescapable. As she later wrote of her portraiture, 'I think that for a picture to represent the Queen it was necessary to have it serious.'[16]

For a decade photographs of the royal couple repeated the same story, careful studies in torpid ordinariness. This black-and-white Victoria is a woman of uncertain dress sense and unlovely appearance, with her weak chin, amphibious glare and stolid expression; Albert broods, sternly attentive. Although photographs of the royal family were not publicly displayed until May 1857, images of this sort had been engraved in periodicals for some time, disseminating the happy family album. In May 1842, *The Illustrated London News* claimed, 'Queen Victoria will never appear more exalted in the world's opinion than when each side of the picture is . . . revealed – the great Queen and stateswoman in the gorgeous palace – the young, lovely and virtuous mother amidst the pure joys of sylvan retreat and domestic relaxation.'[17] In the following decade, the paper expanded its focus to Victoria's children.[18]

Today it is easy to overlook the radicalism of this

calculated embracing of the present. Then as now the camera's truthfulness in conveying its sitters' message was selective. 'Realistic' impressions of an ideal that was never fully realised, Victoria and Albert's photographic portraits broadcast to a watching nation the felicitous domesticity of this family of eleven newly installed in their 'family' homes of Osborne and Balmoral, the former the first of Victoria's houses to include children's bathrooms served by hot and cold water, both practicable only since the spread of the railways. It was Albert's riposte to memories of Victoria's uncles, with their paunchy dysfunctionalism and irregular liaisons. His own father had embraced serial infidelities and adultery had forced his mother's banishment; his only brother contracted syphilis in a career of determined philandering. Albert's distaste for sexual incontinence and the havoc that churned in its wake was acute. The worship of home life banished that divisive spectre. It did something too to balance initial concerns at the size and expense of a dynasty so lavishly endowed with progeny.

Like a careful housewife, Albert supervised the royal purse strings, thrift an appropriately middle-class virtue with which to regulate this masquerade of homeliness. To fund Blore and Cubitt's extension and renovation of Buckingham Palace, the Brighton Pavilion was sold. It smacked too vividly of the Regent's peacock bibulousness and fleshy excess to satisfy Victoria and Albert's quite different aspirations; some of its furnishings were recycled. Albert rationalised the running of the Queen's households, imposing order in place of a cumbrousness hijacked by absentee sinecures, syncopated government departments and potty traditions; Lehzen became his first victim. She departed for Bückeburg and a quiet life with her sister on 30 September 1842, accused of meddling and ineptness.

Victoria wept, but quickly regained her composure; the pension she granted her 'dearest' Lehzen was generous but not so generous as that bestowed on Sir John Conroy. In the autumn of 1852, the Privy Purse was further swelled by an unexpected windfall of half a million pounds from an eccentric miser with a *tendresse* for Victoria, John Camden Nield. (Newspapers wrongly predicted that Victoria would not touch a single coin but give it all to charity. *Lloyd's Weekly Newspaper* outlined needier causes than the Queen.[19] Victoria had other ideas, comforting herself that Nield had known she 'would not waste it'.) In a period of extreme suffering for so many of Victoria's subjects, Albert's financial common sense and the couple's 'normal' family life helped defuse the potentially sensitive issue of significant royal spending on Osborne and Balmoral (Victoria's bill for Osborne alone ultimately reached £200,000 [20]).

Their happy family life, however, was always in part a convenient fiction, like those eternally sunny turquoise skies supplied on request by Winterhalter as a background to the family portraits. It overlooked those separations between parents and children imposed by Victoria's position. It ignored the time the children spent in the company of other adults: nurses, governesses and tutors, variable in their sympathies. Most of all, it obfuscated the nature of Victoria's own pleasure in her family, her occasionally limited enjoyment of the company of her children individually, her resentment of the part unwittingly played by those children in diminishing further 'the rare happiness of being alone with my beloved Albert'.[21] For his part, the high-minded Albert *was* capable of playfulness towards his children and embraced the rough and tumble of childrearing with greater conviction than Victoria, turning somersaults in the haystacks of the

Osborne fields at harvest time, for example. The Swiss Cottage at Osborne was Albert's inspiration: today it stands as a symbol of that large and loving family of princes and princesses. Happily its miniaturised domesticity accommodated opportunities for learning and its wooden walls were inscribed with improving quotations in German, including, 'You will carry your load more easily if you add patience to the burden', a killjoy coda to lives of privilege. For it was Albert, too, who oversaw for his elder children exacting educational regimes fine-tuned by Stockmar: among their objectives was 'the submission to the supervision & authority of one person for the Development of Character' – an unwritten principle of his own relationship with Victoria.[22] Victoria deferred to his judgement, and neither husband nor wife heeded Melbourne's advice that education 'may be able to do much, but it does not do so much as is expected from it. It may mould and direct the character but it rarely changes it.'[23] That shortsightedness blighted the growing up of several of the royal children, none more than Bertie, whom his mother decried as her 'caricature'. Aware of her own shortcomings, she tolerated Albert whipping their eldest son and Stockmar's constant fault-finding with the boy. For Victoria cherished no higher aspiration than that her children should emulate their father: most eventually preferred her path of flawed obstinacy and kindly hauteur. But Albert is markedly absent from those albums of sketches in which, through two decades, Victoria commemorated the idle moments of her vigorous brood. She offered posterity no explanation for the omission.

Albert's martinet tendency was central to his mirthless concept of duty. He applied the same rigorous standards to himself, perpetually selflessly in pursuit of self-improvement, and also to Victoria. 'I have become extremely pleased with Victoria during the past few months. She has only twice had the sulks . . . She puts more confidence in me daily,' he had written to his brother Ernest in September 1840.[24] The couple had been married less than a year; Victoria was two months away from giving birth to their first child. Already in Albert's letter the expectant mother occupied the role of child in her relationship with her 'perfect' husband: appraised, painstakingly corrected, found wanting or commended, her submission growing. In the 'Angel's' treatment of his spirited young wife were pedantry and a degree of detachment at odds with Victoria's effulgent idolisation. 'If only,' he wrote, 'you were rather less occupied with yourself and your feelings . . .'[25] He recoiled from the *Sturm und Drang* of Victoria's unregulated emotions, the magnificent self-indulgence of her anger – ironically, given that Victoria herself traced the origin of her passionate nature and uncontrollable temper to Augusta, Duchess of Saxe-Coburg-Saalfeld, the grandmother whom she and Albert shared. At intervals he would treat his children with similar exactingness. It is a measure of Victoria's love for Albert, as well as the limitations of her self-confidence and the strength of prevailing ideas about the respective roles of men and women, that she responded without effrontery to treatment that with hindsight suggests systematic undermining. Victoria's continuing willingness to play Galatea to Albert's Pygmalion became a prerequisite for their married bliss. In time she noticed it only to applaud it.

It would be wrong to discount love. Nothing suggests that Albert's affection for Victoria ever attained the tsunami-like force of Victoria's own feelings: it did not need to. Yet theirs *was* a relationship centred on reciprocity, albeit Albert found it easier to reciprocate Victoria's feelings when she behaved in a fashion he condoned. Sir Robert Peel, we know, had earlier remarked on Victoria's 'manner . . ., her apparent deep sense of her situation, and . . . her firmness'. The didactic aspect of Albert's love lessened neither his wife's firmness nor her deep sense of her unique position, but he tamed her manner, especially towards himself. The pill was carefully sugared. During the fortnight Victoria remained in bed after the birth of their first child, she eulogised his care for her as 'like that of a mother, nor could there be a kinder, wiser, or more judicious nurse',[26] one of several references to Albert as her 'mother'. It is indicative of the trust she placed in him and, in part, of the nature of the feelings he inspired in her. It suggests too vulnerability beneath her royal bombast, a lapse which would develop into full-scale dependency. She 'leant on him for all and everything – without [him] I did nothing, moved not a finger, arranged not a print or photograph, didn't put on a gown or bonnet if he didn't approve it'. After his death, Victoria itemised the nature of his supremacy, lamenting the loss of 'his pure and perfect spirit . . . guiding and leading me and inspiring me', herself always the object, never the subject, of those dominant 'Albertine' participles.[27] In the same way, communications with ministers and memoranda on government policy, copied out in Victoria's hand, issued mostly from Albert's, not Victoria's, unflagging pen. Albert's thoughts became Victoria's, Victoria's influence on government Albert's influence. Victoria's monarchy was moulded by Albert's conception of a vigorous, engaged sovereign involved with every aspect of policy: informed, consulted and, ultimately, attended to. It was surely as Albert had always intended, though hardly the version of sovereignty the *Manchester Guardian* had in mind for Victoria in 1837 when it welcomed her accession as that of a monarch shaped by the discourse of the 1832 Reform Act.

Victoria and Albert did not ignore the brave new world around them. Their visits to the industrial cities of the north and the Midlands signalled a gear shift in royal practice. Melbourne, whose ministry finally fell in 1841, had dampened Victoria's enthusiasm for *Oliver Twist*, deploring depictions of wretchedness, and dismissed with flippancy her questions concerning the fate of evicted Irish tenantry. Disdainfully he lamented the affectation of the middle classes, whom he professed to dislike. (*The Times*, by contrast, in 1844 referred to 'the middle classes, who may now almost be considered the ruling class of England'.[28]) Victoria and Albert symbolically embraced these representatives of an emerging order. Under Albert's tutelage, Victoria learnt to recognise the qualities of Melbourne's successor, Sir Robert Peel, himself a man of manufacturing stock. Amid waving flags and cheering crowds in Manchester or Liverpool, husband and wife congratulated barrel-chested merchants and rubicund industrialists; they shook hands with councillors and corporations, listened to tens of thousands of Sunday School children drilled in the National Anthem, and knighted the mayors who welcomed them. But they did something more, too, as we have seen, for in rebranding the monarchy they sought out common ground with those men and women whose lives of provincial endeavour so greatly differed from their own.

It may have tended to their own benefit. Victoria justified her throne in terms of proximity to the divinity and advocated for her subjects, as she told Lord John Russell in 1848, 'obedience to the laws and to the Sovereign', 'obedience to a higher Power, divinely instituted for the good of the people'.[29] This unassailable confidence came less easily to Albert, the penniless offshoot of a gimcrack Saxon crown. He dreamt of an active, effective throne, in the vanguard of enlightened patronage and liberal thinking for the good of the world. He dreamt of a united Germany irradiated by political liberalism, a natural partner for Britain, solid and reliable between volatile France and Russian despotism. He dreamt of Britain and Germany together, showering the blessings of justice, reason – in the form of constitutional government – and peace on an unenlightened continent: to that shimmering chimera he eventually sacrificed his favourite daughter. He dreamt . . . and not content with dreaming he did . . . and then he did more. He worked unceasingly. As he wrote to his brother Ernest on 6 April 1861, 'I go on working at my treadmill, as life seems to me.'[30] In pursuit of that boyhood espousal of usefulness, Albert's habit of remorseless service began early in his marriage; in time he simply tired himself out. In his beginning was his end.

There were compensations along the way. The overwhelming success in 1851 of The Great Exhibition of the Works of Industry of All Nations saw Albert acclaimed as an individual of superhuman power. 'By a wizard's rod/ A blazing arch of lucid glass/ Leaps like a fountain from the grass/ To meet the sun!', Thackeray wrote of the Crystal Palace, packed full of tens of thousands of gaudy and grandiose exhibits. On a heroic scale, worthiness and earnest aspiration were displayed together in Paxton's magnificent glass structure, which sought to represent the world and enforce amity through trade. Its opening ceremony became 'the *happiest, proudest* day' of Victoria's life. 'Albert's dearest name is immortalised with this *great* conception, *his* own, and my *own* dear country *showed* she was *worthy* of it.'[31] Even in the glow of Albert's triumph Victoria attested the deceit of the dual monarchy: while the Exhibition was all Albert's doing, the country that acknowledged its success belonged to Victoria. It was the language of entitlement and Albert remained excluded. In the public mind he was still his wife's subordinate.

Victoria's own sterling qualities were stimulated not by dreams of peace but the nightmarish actuality of war. On 28 February 1854, the 1st Battalion Scots Fusilier Guards gathered at Buckingham Palace to present arms before the Queen. They 'gave three hearty cheers, which went to my heart', Victoria recorded in her journal. 'May God protect these fine men, may they be preserved and victorious.' The soldiers were on the eve of departure for the Black Sea and a war, declared that day, which would highlight vividly the shortcomings of Britain's armed forces, shocking inadequacies in the chains of command and supply. From the inglorious and ill-conceived progress of the Crimean War emerged the legend of Florence Nightingale and the 'noble six hundred' of Tennyson's 'Charge of the Light Brigade'; it hastened overdue army reforms and new-minted the bond between sovereign and troops.

In her country's bid to defeat the Tsar of Russia's determination to entrust to the Orthodox Church guardianship of the Holy Places in Jerusalem – itself understood as a metaphor for Russian expansionist tendencies towards the crumbling Ottoman Empire – Victoria became obsessively martial. 'Exceedingly' she regretted that her sex prevented her from fighting. She was frantic for news of the war's progress. To Leopold she wrote on 13 October 1854, 'We are, and indeed the whole country is, *entirely* engrossed with one idea, one *anxious* thought – the *Crimea*.'[32] She regarded the troops with maternal propriety: like a mother she brooded on their youth and 'the entire want of all method and arrangement in everything which concerns [their] comfort'.[33] Her fury at 'the *arrogant* and *dangerous pretensions* of that *barbarous power* Russia'[34] was unbounded. Temporarily her instinct for tub-thumping exceeded even that of the Prime Minister who for almost a decade had been a thorn in her side, Henry Temple, 3rd Viscount Palmerston. Egotistical, arrogant, at heart a Regency buck and high-handed to boot, with a calculated recklessness which repeatedly endeared him to an electorate smug with chauvinism, Palmerston had previously frittered limited energy in winning Victoria's good graces. At a moment of national crisis, monarch and minister found common ground. Victoria suggested the motto of a new medal, the Victoria Cross: 'For Valour'. She also presented in person Crimean service medals to veterans regardless of rank. 'The rough hand of the brave and honest private soldier came for the first time in contact with that of the Sovereign and their Queen,' she wrote.[35] She confessed to feeling 'as if they were *my own children*'.[36]

The war had been fought alongside the French. State visits from and to Napoleon III and the Empress Eugénie cemented this uneasy alliance between old enemies. At the tomb of the first Napoleon in the chapel of the Hôtel des Invalides, listening to 'God Save the Queen' by torchlight as thunder crashed outside, Napoleon III seduced Victoria with an instinct for drama and his lickspittle charm; the Empress delighted her sturdy guest with her chic and her dolorous beauty. Eugénie introduced the crinoline to Britain, a frou-frou distraction at a time of unsatisfactory war. In return Victoria astonished Parisian eyes with a series of sartorial surprises: a bright green umbrella, an oversize handbag embroidered with a sequinned poodle and a '[Paris-made] white net dress embroidered with gold and trimmed with red geraniums, and (as were all my evening dresses) very full', which the Emperor assumed was of English design.[37] The figure she cut was that once described by the novelist Charlotte Brontë: 'She looked a little stout vivacious lady . . . not much . . . pretension about her.'[38] Yet observers on both sides of the Channel agreed that, of the two women, Victoria was the more truly regal. When at last, in March 1856, peace broke out, it brought with it little victory for the Queen whose attitude of unwavering belligerence had suggested a second Elizabeth. Lugubriously she dismissed the entire year as 'gloomy'. On the horizon she may have imagined she discerned bright spots, the war concluded, the happy yearly round of Windsor Castle, Osborne and Balmoral again upon its course. In one of those moments of stock-taking in which she habitually indulged in her journal, she had lately assessed her own advance towards that state of ideal personal development advocated by Albert: she celebrated 'the happy conviction that I have made great progress and am trying energetically to overcome my faults'. Her gratitude, of course, sought out her husband who made all things possible: 'How can I thank my dearest Albert for his unchanging love and wonderful tenderness . . .'[39]

She was unable to glimpse the future. There was worse to come.

6

'The pain of parting'

To her journal, Victoria had confided her desire that the clock stop. 'When one is as happy as we, one feels sad at the quick passing of the years, & I always wish Time could stand still for a while.'[1] She was contented and fulfilled. She asked only that nothing should change, that this bud of happiness should open unfettered and blossom for ever, no worm within it. It was not to be.

As the 1850s drew to a close, Victoria suffered a loss in her close family. In this instance it was a loss which became a gain. The marriage of her eldest daughter, Vicky, Princess Royal, to Prince Frederick William of Prussia, called Fritz, took place on 25 January 1858. Afterwards prince and princess departed for Potsdam and Berlin and a life in which, as Victoria observed, military uniforms were worn day long and, as Vicky noted, the plumbing did not suit. Vicky was seventeen: 'all the childish roundness still clung to her', recorded her new Prussian lady-in-waiting.[2] She was emotionally young too. A flotilla of her mother's letters pursued her across the chill wastes of the North Sea: for forty years they would flow unstaunched. In the long term, Vicky's absence provided Victoria with the most significant of several epistolary relationships. In

the short term, it inspired first essays in the language of
abandonment, that lexicon she soon mastered with maudlin
but determined relish. Victoria acclaimed her eldest
daughter as 'the object of our tenderest solicitude for 17
years':[3] her written response to their parting suggests
inconvenience over broken-heartedness, and her thoughts
were not so much solicitous as peevish. 'And now I must
end, my beloved child, the separation from whom I can
not accustom myself to – and at times get quite angry
about it. I think it quite wrong you should have been
carried off.'[4] Recrimination coloured regret. With more
conviction, and foolhardy tactlessness, Vicky responded to
her mother's initial tears by addressing herself to Albert:
'The pain of parting from you yesterday was greater than
I can describe . . . I miss you so dreadfully, dear Papa,
more than I can say . . .'[5] Yet it was Albert who had let
this daughter go, Albert's plan, his vision. She was his
protégée and a prodigy to boot. As he had tamed Victoria
and reformed the throne of England, so would Vicky help
Fritz bring light into the militant darkness of militarist
Prussia, a conduit for her father's intransigent benignity.
As it fell out, death shielded Albert from the unravelling
of his plans and the chasm of unhappiness into which
opinionated but well-intentioned Vicky, 'always clever,
never wise', rapidly blundered. It was Victoria who
survived to witness joy give way to tragedy.

The Prussian marriage was the single great dynastic
union forged by a child of Victoria and Albert. Stockmar
encouraged the scheme, Leopold too; in John Philip's
painting of the marriage service, Leopold is surely
whispering in Albert's ear, attentive at his nephew's shoulder.
Albert was motivated by idealism: his airy plan became as
dandelion clocks in the harsh blast of Bismarck's cynicism.
Victoria shared his dream. On a less exalted level, in

intervals between harrying and chiding, she enjoyed Vicky's promotion to the status of grown-up with whom she could exchange confidences and reflections on the lot of wives and mothers. It was ironic that only through separation did mother and daughter discover the intimacy and easy devotedness which had eluded them so often during Vicky's childhood, letters – even from Victoria's forceful pen – more emollient than the reality of daily contact. Not for the last time Victoria succeeded in her own mind in bringing order to a disorderly relationship by committing that relationship to paper, its dialectic safely confined within the bounds of her own writing. She expressed herself with characteristic frankness in the first summer of Vicky's absence: 'Doubt your real affection and your love, I did not, dearest child – but you did all you could to make me doubt it; for a more insubordinate and more unequal-tempered child and girl I think I never saw!'[6] So easily in Victoria's mind was the score settled and laid aside.

From its first clandestine flickerings, when, in September 1855, Fritz acknowledged to her parents that he was in love with the fourteen-year-old Vicky, it was an engagement that provoked a bittersweet response in Victoria. Her sense of Vicky's extreme youth augmented what would become her standard reaction to the idea of girls' marriage: an overwhelming aversion, despite the happiness of her own conjugal relations, to the coming union's sexual implications ('I said to Papa . . . "after all, it is like taking a poor lamb to be sacrificed"'[7]). Credits to balance so unsettling a debit included Victoria's personal fondness for Fritz, the thrill this essentially romantic woman derived from her daughter's evident adoration of her handsome prince, and her pride in Albert's plans for Continental constitutionalism. It was also a connection of suitable éclat, though Victoria was clear that it was her own family which added lustre to the bargain. 'Whatever may be the usual practice of Prussian Princes, it is not *every* day that one marries the eldest daughter of the Queen of England,' she thundered over inevitable pre-wedding glitches. It was an assertion that did not invite correction.

Victoria was in a state of unsettlement. Sir James Clark, who remained her physician despite the fiasco of the Flora Hastings Affair and any number of subsequent misdiagnoses, had insisted that her latest baby, Beatrice, be her last. Clark shared Albert's mistaken fear that Victoria's predisposition to postnatal depression presaged mental illness of the sort that had so dramatically incapacitated her grandfather George III. In addition, intimations of mortality began their surefooted approach. On 10 December 1857, Victoire, Duchesse de Nemours, a first cousin of both Victoria and Albert through her father Ferdinand of Saxe-Coburg, died in childbirth, the second of Victoria's cousins to die in the same house of the same cause. She was thirty-five years old, beautiful, quiet and unobtrusive. A daughter-in-law of the exiled King Louis Philippe of France, she had lived at Claremont and enjoyed an easy intimacy with the British royal couple: Victoria described her as 'like a dear sister to us'. Certainly the cousins' closeness was such that Victoria and Albert viewed her body after death. Startlingly Albert recorded his impressions. She was 'pale and rigid, but like an angel of beauty, her glorious hair falling in waves over her bosom', a response evocative of its time.[8] In its unflinching focus and apparent sensuousness, Albert's description foreshadows that preoccupation with death and its mysteries which would all too soon envelop Victoria's life.

* * *

On 6 December 1839, Albert had outlined in a letter the very mixed emotions he felt on contemplating his final departure from Coburg to marry Victoria. The recipient of that letter was Victoria's mother.

The Duchess of Kent was Albert's paternal aunt, called by him 'Aunt Kent', like him a Coburger in England. They had met in 1836 and again in 1839. Despite the breakdown in Victoria's own relationship with her mother, Albert's letter was open and familiar. 'I am lost in bewilderment,' he told his aunt, an invitation for complicity. At the outset, the Duchess apparently had reason to resent her nephew: his marriage to Victoria provided the latter with the excuse she craved for removing her mother from Buckingham Palace. Yet the arrival of Albert was to spell the beginning of a rapprochement between the two women. Victoria herself had done nothing to achieve this: the Duchess at least had previously asked advice of the Duke of Wellington on a possible solution to so acrimonious an impasse.

Albert may have been guided by fondness for his aunt, her tendency to behave in a manner that was foolish, vain, conniving and meddlesome notwithstanding. His behaviour betrayed that family feeling which was embedded in the Coburg psyche, the same feeling which later shaped his attitude to his children and, in time, helped inspire Victoria's spiderweb orchestration of a Europe-wide matriarchy. His motives also included expediency. Albert sought and identified the cause of Victoria's continuing enmity towards her mother. By happy chance he found it in his own bête noire, Baroness Lehzen. Albert had not long been married to Victoria before he managed Lehzen's low-key dismissal. He was certain that the retirement of this gossiping and over-ambitious ex-governess, so essential to his own happiness, would increase Victoria's happiness too by eliminating the principal remaining agent of discord between mother and daughter.

And so it proved to be, though Victoria, in many ways free from guile, was adept at nurturing dislike and slow to exonerate those who had angered her. In this instance she appeared unable fully to grasp the extent and nature of the Duchess's love for her, but dutifully made available to her mother Clarence House in London and Frogmore Lodge, Windsor, both of which had stood empty since the death of her aunt, Princess Augusta, in September 1840. The process of relocation was successful: separation did indeed make the heart grow fonder in Victoria's case. The way was cleared for the Duchess's metamorphosis into much-loved grandmother. As a portrait sketch of 1851 by Henry Courtney Selous and Winterhalter's oval portrait of 1857 make clear, the older woman was in nowise changed: the compressed lips and unflinching gaze of both images testify to steadiness of purpose and a firmness to match her daughter's.

The Duchess's diary for 18 June 1857 recorded the experience of sitting for Winterhalter for the last time: 'It is a great penitence for me to sit for my picture, but it is for Victoria. It made me very tired.'[9] The Duchess was seventy-one and her energies fading; Victoria commended only her mother's youthfulness of spirit, which she summoned for the sake of her grandchildren. Lady-in-waiting Lady Augusta Bruce, observing the Duchess at close quarters, chronicled her decline less evasively. 'It goes to one's heart to see one symptom after another and increasing discomfort and inconvenience,' she wrote on 15 January 1861.[10] Her death on 16 March, a week after an operation on her arm, did not greatly surprise. But its effect on Victoria was elemental. Initial physical collapse gave way to a nervous breakdown so overwhelming that rumours of her insanity swept the chancelleries of Europe; in Prussia Vicky could not escape the clamour of septic whispers. Victoria was crushed by grief. Guilt played its part, impossible that it should not. Remorse too. Her journal offered agonising reading. 'I don't believe Ma. ever really loved me,' she had written, reporting a conversation with Melbourne.[11] She must once have believed it, and perhaps subsequently too. To tears for her mother were added tears for herself, for her misapprehension, the misconstructions, the injustice of her angry folly; tears for what had vanished never to be recalled; tears for what might have been; tears for the happy times; tears on top of tears. 'The relief of tears is great,' she wrote to Vicky on 10 April, 'they come again and again every day and are soothing to the bruised heart and soul.'[12] Although Victoria fled the jarring company of her family in order to find solace in solitude and silence, her tears would not soon be dried. Ominously she insisted three days later, 'I love to dwell on her . . . and not to be roused out of my grief!'[13] Later she claimed that 'the power of enjoyment of any thing seems (for the time) entirely gone!'[14] In truth she had discovered an alternative enjoyment, this only child of forty-one who, remarkably in the middle years of the nineteenth century, had never previously encountered the reality of death so nearly.

It was a foretaste of things to come.

Vicky soon fell pregnant. To the latter's irritation, her mother was unable to be present at the birth. Instead Victoria and Albert visited their married daughter months before the great event. For both, there were already indications that Vicky would fail in her 'civilising' mission to Prussia: 'I always feel like a fly struggling in a very tangled web, and a feeling of weariness and depression, often of disgust and hopelessness, takes possession of me,' Vicky lamented.[15] Her parents ignored the signs. In her journal Victoria recorded details of a more picturesque variety. The customs of Prussian mourning struck her forcibly, the habit of preserving undisturbed souvenirs of the departed: the chair in which Frederick the Great had died darkened still with bloody stains.[16] At home she revisited 'unhappy Claremont' a year after Victoire's death. In a handsome display case she saw her cousin's hair – preserved under glass in all its serpentine lustrousness. The finality of death seemed simultaneously to be celebrated and denied. For Victoria, deep in her subconscious, a picture was forming.

Albert's death on 14 December 1861, though he was only forty-two, ought to have been no more surprising than that of the Duchess of Kent, but Victoria was skilful in resisting the unpalatable. Freely she acknowledged her husband's physical exhaustion, his sleeplessness too and the all-encompassing depression which further sapped his energies (it also sapped his will to live, though Victoria did not care to dwell on his more fatalistic utterances). Since she knew only too well that she could not survive without him, she refused to countenance that possibility. The irredeemably unreliable Clark, at seventy-three still forceful in his ineptitude, appeared to bolster her breezy attitude: he refused the assistance of colleagues and lulled the willing Victoria into a state of denial which surprised some onlookers. A grim sort of comedy is injected into Housman's *Death and the Doctors* by Clark's equivocation. Albert, he allows, is ill: 'dangerously' ill – the qualification suggested by a solicitous Princess Alice as a means of preparing Victoria for every eventuality – is a description too

A sentimental image of dynastic intent, William Beechey's portrait of the infant Victoria with her mother, the Duchess of Kent, asserts her right to rule: in her hand she clasps a miniature of her deceased father.

'Striking ... though not entirely correct' was Victoria's assessment of the first of Henry Tanworth Wells' paintings of the moment the Archbishop of Canterbury and the Lord Chamberlain informed her of her accession on 20 June 1837. Wells' painting – undertaken fifty years later – is a romantic reimagining of that 'historical incident'.

In this unabashedly regal portrait of 1843, Francis Grant references only Victoria's role as queen.

A youthful Victoria is depicted in an informal setting surrounded by flowers in the second year of her reign.

On different occasions Victoria dismissed official portraits of the 'dear Being' Lord Melbourne as 'too old and not handsome enough' and 'not in my opinion half pleasing enough'. Here she attempted her own sketch of her first, best-loved prime minister.

Prussian sculptor Emil Wolff depicted Albert as a Greek warrior. Victoria thought it 'very beautiful' but Albert later commissioned a second, less 'undressed' version.

At the first of the three great fancy dress balls given by Victoria, on 12 May 1842 she appeared as Queen Philippa, Albert as Edward III. Her costume, here recorded for posterity by Landseer, was based on the Westminster Abbey tomb effigy of the medieval queen, on which Edward, famously devoted to his bride, lavished £3,000 in 1369.

In words and pictures, the popular press dwelt on the royal couple's conspicuous happiness and domestic bliss.

In 1845, Victoria paid Franz Xaver Winterhalter £105 for this group portrait in which she appears alongside her four eldest children (from left: the Princess Royal, Princess Alice, Prince Alfred and the Prince of Wales).

Victoria's own badge of the Order of Victoria and Albert, *c.*1862–3, on which, uniquely, the position of the portraits of husband and wife was reversed.

Photographs like this one, depicting Victoria with Alice and Louise and a portrait of the recently deceased Albert, encouraged some observers to discern in her mourning a theatrical dimension.

In Victoria's mind a picture of shadows – 'as I am now, sad & lonely' – Landseer's famous *Her Majesty at Osborne in 1866* gave rise to ribald comment on public exhibition at the Royal Academy in 1867.

The widowed Victoria at one of her collection of spinning wheels, an unsympathetic image of stolidly unrelenting gloom.

Victoria
commissioned
Tuxen's
sumptuous
group portrait to
commemorate
the family
gathering of her
Golden Jubilee
in 1887.

At the end of
her life, Victoria
declined
to grant
Jean Joseph
Benjamin-
Constant
proper sittings.
His portrait of
1899 has an
ethereal quality,
which seems
to foreshadow
Victoria's
death as well as
investing her
with intimations
of immortality.

frightening for Clark to permit. And so the prince dies, killed by highhandedness in the matter of adverbs.

To Vicky, on 27 November 1861, Victoria claimed that Albert was suffering from 'a cold with neuralgia'. This was exacerbated, she explained, by 'loss of rest at night (worse than he has ever had before) . . . caused by a great sorrow and worry'.[17] The sorrow in question arose from the deaths from typhoid fever early in the month of twenty-three-year-old King Pedro V of Portugal, eulogised by Victoria as 'out and out *the* most distinguished young Prince there is . . . good, excellent and steady, according to one's heart's desire',[18] and his brother Prince Ferdinand; both were the sons of a Coburg cousin, and Victoria likened Albert's love for Pedro to that of a father. The source of the worry was Albert's own son, Bertie. In medical terms, neither could be categorised as a cause of death, although the egregious Clark would make just that connection, afterwards citing Bertie's love affair as a nail in Albert's coffin.[19] Both he and his successor William Jenner also pinpointed Albert's excessive workload. Jenner's assessment that it was 'great worry, and far too hard work for too long' was one Victoria would afterwards exploit to the full. [20]

In 1849, the Prussian sculptor Emil Wolff had completed a second version of a statue of Albert dressed in the garb of a Greek warrior.[21] Although Victoria had commended the first version as 'very beautiful', Albert recoiled from the exposure of his marble limbs, barefoot and wearing the shortest of filmy 'kilts' beneath his breastplate. He regarded it as 'too undressed'. He commissioned a revised study, which was afterwards displayed at Buckingham Palace in company with a similarly Greek representation of Victoria. In Wolff's second statue, Albert wears sandals. His kilt too is demonstrably longer. Propriety had been restored and modesty defended; so painstakingly was eroticism banished. It was indicative of the need for unwavering vigilance: ironic indeed had Albert's own portraiture celebrated fleshly indulgence.

But it is easier to modify the appearance of a work of art than the inclinations of a young man of easygoing bonhomie exposed to the full panoply of worldly temptations. Only the highest expectations had ever been cherished for the Prince of Wales. For Albert, his eldest son must become a model prince, living proof of the thoroughness of Albert's own cleansing of the Augean Stable that was England's Hanoverian court; to that end, from earliest infancy Bertie had been 'entrusted to persons only who [were] themselves morally good, intelligent, well-informed and experienced'.[22] For Victoria he must emulate in every way the perfect and angelic father whose name he shared. 'I wish that he should grow up *entirely* under *his Father's eye*, and *every* step be *guided* by him, so that when he has attained the age of 16 or 17 he may be a real companion to his Father,' Victoria stated when Bertie was three.[23] Neither parent took much account of Bertie's own nature. He was a cipher, a blank tablet on which their palpably good intentions could be deeply graven. Predictably he proved a disappointment to them both.

His fall, when it happened, involved a young woman of pert allure and elastic morals called Nellie Clifden. An unremarkable example of wild oats, it provoked in Albert – this man whose punctiliousness extended even to the undress of a statue – an overreaction of hysterical proportions, as if like a comet's tail Bertie's casual transgression summoned from some shady underworld all the indiscriminate lasciviousness of recent royal history. His mercy dash to Cambridge to rescue the twenty-year-old heir to the throne tired and weakened a man already sickening. Only days earlier, Albert had visited the new Staff College at Sandhurst on a morning of persistent rain. In Cambridge, father and son were reconciled during a lengthy walk also conducted in intermittent biting rain.

Albert had complained of rheumatism, of aching limbs which sharpened his tiredness. He was always cold. When, before first light, he began his self-appointed task of never-ending paperwork, he resorted to a wig to warm that bald patch which contributed to his prematurely aged appearance. The robust and bustling Victoria was torn between irritation and a desperate sort of sympathy, anxious that Albert had simply given up. At intervals he had told her as much. 'He had suddenly grown weary in the middle of his days . . . he was tired, though it was still noonday and life seemed yet to stretch far before him.'[24]

More than 150 years after the event, the two-week countdown to Albert's death retains an unreal quality, as if the players in this drama are each reading from separate scripts, wilful in their adherence to the certainty of conflicting outcomes. On 30 November, and 4, 6, 10 and 11 December, Victoria wrote to Vicky to reassure her daughter that Albert's condition was improving; on 2 and 7 December, her letters indicated 'a sort of feverish attack'. Only on 13 December, did Fritz receive a telegram instructing him to prepare his pregnant wife for worse news, by then less than a day away.

The royal doctors misled Victoria, incompetence to agree an effective course of treatment compounded by their desire to avoid, at all costs, a second collapse of the sort she had endured following the death of the Duchess; 'no cause for alarm', Clark asserted, must be their mantra if Victoria were not to buckle under the strain.[25] Torn between her determination to believe them and the daily evidence of

Albert's lassitude and listlessness, his loss of appetite and inability to rally strength, Victoria oscillated between prostration and a tremulous conviction of imminent recovery. Her need for Albert remained overwhelming: it demanded the empty nourishment contained in the doctors' evasive diagnosis of 'gastric fever'. But her terror never left her, all too clear to that grown-up daughter, Alice, who at this moment of crisis acted as nurse to both parents. Sometimes Victoria's fears expressed themselves in exasperation. Albert in return behaved unpredictably towards his wife, repeatedly irascible; there were interludes of tenderness. At her father's request, Alice played hymns: 'To Thee, O Lord, I yield my spirit/ Who break'st, in love, this mortal chain;/ My life I but from Thee inherit,/ And death becomes my chiefest gain.'[26] It was not a happy choice. By a tremendous effort, he had undertaken one final piece of work on his wife's behalf, modifying the stridency of an ultimatum which the government meant to deliver to their American counterparts. America was embroiled in civil war: without Albert's intervention in the matter of the illegal boarding of a British ship, Britain too might have found herself party to that conflagration. Handing over the draft, Albert told Victoria, 'I am so weak, I have hardly been able to hold the pen', words without exaggeration. Husband and wife were locked in a spiral of sleeplessness from which only one would emerge.

Belatedly bulletins alerted the public to Albert's ill health. They avoided the only issue that mattered, a truthful assessment of the likelihood or otherwise of the prince's recovery from typhoid fever. On the final day, only three days after Victoria had written to Vicky, 'I can, I am thankful to say, report another good night . . . The doctors are satisfied . . . he is not weaker,'[27] Albert's black and swollen tongue struggled to form even the names of those he loved. At the end there were no parting words for the wife who hung on his every word, no intimacy in a room crowded with relatives and retainers, save Victoria's unremitting focus on the man she loved with desperate urgency. She held his hand in hers, though it was already cold. She would not let go.

7

'Unavailing regrets'

THE TIMES WAS quite mistaken when, in the aftermath of Albert's death, it asserted as a certainty: 'We have on the throne a Sovereign whose nerves have been braced rather than paralysed by the chill of adversity.'[1] If only Victoria could have responded to that hearty profession, as she would later (albeit anonymously) respond to such assertions on the newspapers' parts, she might have indicated with some vigour how inadequate was its description of her suffering. In virtual seclusion at Osborne, attended by her daughter Alice, heedless of the passing days, of Christmas which came and went without joyful intermission, she concerned herself with thoughts of Albert, 'of his great goodness and purity, quite unlike anyone else', her existence 'as if living in a dreadful dream', 'like life in death',[2] those thoughts, as Albert had once warned Vicky, 'much in the past' and guided by 'a spiritual necessity to cling to moments that are flown and to recollections': alone in a grieving nation unmoved by those many tributes of the press which belatedly acknowledged Albert's worth. (It was not until 21 January that Victoria's journal indicates she was aware of the nature of public reaction to the death. At that point her thoughts were as much of herself as of

Albert: 'Even the poor people in small villages, who don't know me, are shedding tears for me . . .'[3]) A nearer and more straightforward assessment than that of *The Times* is contained in the letter Victoria wrote to King William of Prussia on 4 February: 'For me, life came to an end on December 14.'[4]

For almost a century writers, and readers, have treated Victoria with something less than reverence. The arch insinuations of Lytton Strachey's *Queen Victoria*, published in 1921, suggest selfishness and humbug. Strachey quotes Victoria only to tease her as he drags her from her pedestal; he will not allow her sincerity. In Strachey's hands, Victoria's written utterances embody the vices of a generation and a culture. Her lavish underlinings, the exclamation marks she haemorrhages with such emphatic abandon and her perpetually bleeding heart, all goad him to quiet but deadly laughter – oh, the earnestness, the egotism and the vehemence of those Victorians! Post Strachey, readers encounter Victoria ironically; such irony targets the frequently exaggerated idiom in which Victoria expressed herself, never more so than after Albert's death. But in doing so it strips her writing of its power and denies the possibility of her pain. After Albert's death, Victoria did indeed appear to revel in the unfolding narrative of her misery, she herself its foremost chronicler. It ought not to be grounds for surprise.

As long ago as 1839, threatened with the defeat of Melbourne's government, she had exclaimed, 'The state of agony, grief and despair into which this placed me may be easier imagined than described! All all my happiness gone! That happy peaceful life destroyed.'[5] Now she gave way to a degree of self-absorption remarkable in so public a figure – and adversely impressive. Yet the immensity of her initial unhappiness is beyond question. Her need to proclaim her grief in writing – the medium which, through her journal and her correspondence, had served as her principal resource for self-expression since the unhappy Kensington years – was also a means of bringing order to chaos and legitimising those extraordinarily powerful emotions which otherwise threatened to fell her. 'I don't know what I feel,' she wrote to Vicky on 16 December, in a note of affecting incoherence.[6] In letters, her journal and a small notebook, *Remarks – Conversations – Reflections*, she eventually came closer to an answer.

Her reactions on 14 December included dignified acquiescence, as she accepted the condolences and offers of support of her family and her household in the minutes immediately following Albert's death; and the indignity of that agony she could not suppress: she shrieked; like a wounded animal she cried out; attended by a lady-in-waiting she threw herself with open arms on top of Albert's corpse, convulsed with weeping; briefly she lost the use of her legs. Throughout their marriage, Albert had attempted to guide Victoria away from that inclination to excess which he regarded as her family's most dangerous failing. After his death it was the loss of his 'guidance' she lamented most: her reaction was magisterial in its excess. She ordered so much black crepe to drape the rooms and corridors of Windsor Castle that the entire country's store was exhausted: more had to be dyed at speed.[7] She decreed official mourning 'for the longest term in modern times'[8] and barricaded herself in black bombazine: she would wear widow's weeds until the day she died, setting aside into the bargain much of that jewellery designed especially for her by Albert. Her world was hedged in by the thick black margins of that sable-bordered writing paper on which she composed and recomposed the litany of her sorrow, effecting for herself and generations of unintended readers her transformation from Queen of Hearts to Queen of Tears. From the ashes of the pyre emerged the Widow of Windsor.

Occasionally her behaviour bordered on the ludicrous: Privy Council meetings at Osborne, where Victoria sat in an adjoining room, the door ajar, listening but unseen. She observed from vantage points of semi-concealment the marriages of Alice and Bertie – the former to Prince Louis of Hesse in July 1862, the latter, in March of the following year, to Princess Alexandra of Denmark, called Alix, acclaimed by Victoria somewhat vaguely as 'a pearl' and 'a dear lovely being' despite her family's history of immorality, but later deplored for being insufficiently *'grande dame'*.[9] Both matches had been agreed by Albert, who was occupied with the redesign of Bertie and Alix's London house right up until his death. At Alice's wedding in the private apartments at Osborne, Victoria was shielded from onlookers by a human screen formed by her sons, including Alfred, who sobbed conspicuously throughout the ceremony. Above the improvised altar hung Winterhalter's great group portrait, *The Royal Family in 1846*, asserting Albert's presence in spirit and conjuring an alternative Victoria, a figure both maternal and majestic, a contrast which can only have stimulated the curiosity of those present. Afterwards Victoria described the event unapologetically as 'more like a funeral' than a wedding. These tepid festivities represented a poor return for Alice's unfailing sympathy, her nursing and the numerous recent occasions when she had acted as go-between for Victoria and the government ministers she refused to encounter at first hand.

At Bertie's wedding in St George's Chapel, Windsor, Victoria retreated to Catherine of Aragon's closet high above the chancel in the chapel's southeast corner. The combination of the balcony's gold-embroidered velvet draperies and those diamonds which dazzled against Victoria's black weeds did little to render her unobtrusive. (In Frith's painting of the service, it is noticeable that many eyes stray towards Victoria.) Yet this was unintentional on her part. Genuinely she shrank from view. She likened herself to 'a poor hunted hare'.[10] To the unsympathetic it looked like flummery. In her misery she failed to muster many good wishes for Bertie and Alix's happiness, reminded too powerfully of her own vanished joy; instead she concentrated with rapt attention on the less challenging spectacle of her youngest daughter, Albert's last favourite, the five-year-old Beatrice: 'I could not take my eyes off precious little Baby, with her golden hair and large nosegay.' It was self-indulgent . . . it was dampening.

Perhaps she consoled herself that the nation approved her behaviour, as in the aftermath of her mother's death: 'The general sympathy for *me*, and approval of the manner in which I have shown my grief, is *quite wonderful and most touching*.'[11] Almost certainly she was too deeply sunk in wretchedness to care. It does not appear to have occurred to her that the nation's sympathy would prove exhaustible. After its first mistaken assessment, *The Times* granted Victoria a two-year reprieve, before signalling that the time for change was nigh: 'Two years it must be said are a long period to be consumed in unavailing regrets and in dwelling upon days which cannot be healed.'[12] Ever wilful, headstrong to her own detriment and hardwired to resist every form of coercion, Victoria showed no sign of altering her course. Repeatedly *The Times* returned to the fray. From Belgium, Leopold stressed to her the connection between showing herself in public and popular affection. On 26 March 1864, *The Saturday Review* explained, 'Seclusion is one of the few luxuries in which Royal personages may not indulge. The power which is derived from affection or from loyalty needs a life of uninterrupted publicity to sustain it.'[13] Nothing availed. In her husband's memory, on 10 February 1862, the twenty-second anniversary of her wedding, Victoria had instituted a new family order, the Order of Victoria and Albert. The badge consisted of a cameo depicting the heads of husband and wife, Victoria's uppermost, Albert's glimpsed beneath it. When Victoria commissioned the cameo that she herself was to wear, the order of the heads was reversed. It was Albert's which was uppermost, Victoria scarcely visible beneath his classical profile, all but obliterated, a wish made concrete.[14] Talisman-like, Victoria wore the order for the first time at Bertie's wedding. It was obvious what occupied her thoughts.

The public expression of Victoria's widowhood was a contrivance (in private she complained to Vicky, 'I never, never shall be able to bear that dreadful weary, chilling, unnatural life of a widow'[15]). As careful a construct as any of her previous public masquerades, it subsumed Victoria's sovereignty within a domestic role more safely aligned to current sexual politics. In this way alone Victoria clearly acted as Albert's disciple after his death. With more than her usual emphasis, she shared with Leopold her one '*firm* resolve': 'that *his* wishes – *his* plans – about *every* thing are to be *my law!* And *no human power* will make me swerve from *what he* decided and wished.'[16] With that rhetoric of wifely loyalty she kept faith through the next four decades. And yet, as we will see, in invoking Albert's wishes and example, she frequently acted in a manner profoundly 'unAlbertine'. For this daughter of late-Georgian England could not escape her heredity entirely. She was greedy and selfish, albeit the appetites slaked were vanity and pride rather than lust, her extravagance unchecked emotionalism in place of overspending. On 12 October 1863, *The Times* labelled Victoria's grief 'a sort of religion'. In truth it encompassed none of the restraints of conventional religious practice, nearer to the intemperance of a fetish. Victoria's reinvention of herself as tragic heroine perpetuated a distorted, perfected version of Albert's memory. It was an act of piety that, in the short term, was fully comprehensible to many of her contemporaries, with their exuberant mourning and avidity concerning the afterlife. By 1864, dissent was vocal and widespread. Exasperation at Victoria's continuing seclusion undermined her panegyric of 'Albert the Good'. Posterity has inclined to scepticism. The Biblical quotation inscribed in the Albert Memorial Chapel in St George's Chapel, Windsor – 'I have fought the good fight, I have finished my course' – suggests, as Victoria intended, an earthly saint. Smugness too and the chill of perfection.

The broken-hearted Victoria sought solace in a frenzy of artistic patronage. Monuments and memorials to Albert, and the rapid-fire development of a brand new iconography for herself, arose from the same impulse: the need to sanction her grief through consensus concerning Albert's greatness. Over and over Victoria was painted and photographed gazing adoringly at images of Albert; even when the deceased paterfamilias was not visibly represented, Victoria's inky garb or the sorrowing figures of his fatherless children summoned his blameless shade. Significantly, the critic in the *London Review* expressed discomfort at the intimacy of images like William Bambridge's photograph, *Mourning the Prince Consort*, of 1862, in which Victoria and three of her children are posed in attitudes of emotional collapse beside a garlanded bust of the prince; the same critic also hinted with distaste at the degree of theatricality implicit in such artfully contrived tableaux.[17] Such potent public expressions of Victoria's sadness smacked of ostentation. Her detractors recoiled from the apparent relish of her gloom, the orgiastic quality of her suffering.

The dual monarchy of Victoria and Albert had concealed behind closed doors the 'masculine' aspects of Victoria's sovereignty. Instead it publicised her 'hidden', private role as wife and mother. So in the first years of her bereavement, Victoria celebrated this new 'private' role of widow. The wheel had turned full circle: she was again the small child of William Beechey's double portrait, clasping a miniature of her father, herself a pendant to that vanished male. Albert's image by Ross, commissioned in the fervour of her engagement and set in brilliants, served no longer as a badge of possession of all that she had won, but of what was lost. Four decades on, Victoria described herself as 'like a child that has lost its mother'; the Duchess of Atholl described her in her widow's cap as 'look[ing] like a child'.[18] In terms of Victoria the queen, Albert was indeed her progenitor. Observers had noted those occasions when, ventriloquist-like, he instructed Victoria what questions to ask politicians and officials, whispering to her in German at banquets; Victoria then repeated Albert's questions in English. Such puppetry could hardly be made public. While Victoria actively promoted her widowhood, even resorting to being photographed with a spinning wheel in the guise of cottager's relict, roleplay infinitely remote from the political arena she could not escape, she broadcast to a narrower circle and with a degree of circumspection her terror of reigning alone.

Yet terror it was. Albert had insisted that the Crown assert its prerogatives, and had done so on Victoria's behalf.

There were solid grounds for Disraeli's claim that he had 'governed England for twenty-one years with a wisdom and energy such as none of our kings have ever shown'. At his death, Victoria's energy found an alternative outlet; at this stage she lacked the requisite wisdom. She was helpless, like an invalid whose limbs have atrophied from lack of use: suddenly she had to walk unaided.

She begged for assistance: 'It is very difficult for the Queen, when she is left without one word of explanation to assist her, to draw her own conclusions from the perusal of voluminous despatches from abroad . . ., when she receives drafts for her approval, and to judge, in her ignorance of her views of the Government, or of the reasons which have dictated them, whether she should approve them or not.'[19] For she was trapped in a dilemma, longing to exist alone and undisturbed with her grief, determined not to be sidelined by those who sought to downgrade the sovereign's part. As early as 14 January 1862, Victoria reminded the Foreign Secretary of her rights: 'Lord Russell will perhaps take care that the rule should not be departed from, viz that no drafts should be sent without the Queen's having first seen them';[20] the following year she repeated to Palmerston 'her desire that no step is taken in foreign affairs without her previous sanction being obtained'.[21] Before her letter to Russell, she had claimed that she felt 'daily more and more worn and wretched': at the same time she retained the instinct for command. It was the sort of contradiction Victoria regularly embraced. Lady Augusta Bruce, formerly the Duchess of Kent's lady-in-waiting, now a woman of the bedchamber to Victoria, highlighted 'the necessity for Her to act with decision and firmness and the dread lest this should make Her close Her ears to such advice as may yet be offered, but which now no one is in a position to offer'.[22] For the remainder of her long reign, the question of who was in a position to offer advice would exercise not only Victoria but those who felt themselves entrusted with, or entitled to, such a role.

Four days after Albert's death, Victoria wrote to Vicky that she had chosen 'a spot in Frogmore Gardens for a mausoleum for us';[23] a week later she had canvassed her preferred artists for assistance. By the end of the month, Marochetti the sculptor had embarked on the modelling of the head of his tomb effigy of Albert. The building's foundations were begun and, with something like enthusiasm, Victoria anticipated laying the first stone herself in March.

It was a project on which she would lavish considerable attention. The work was costly and time-consuming. Albert's remains were not finally formally interred until 1868, a year after publication of another of Victoria's memorials to her husband, *The Early Years of HRH The Prince Consort*, in which she offered nominal author, equerry Charles Grey, extensive 'assistance'. That lengthy timespan stands as a metaphor for Victoria's state of mind: her reluctance to bury the past and embrace her altered present. In the meantime, she retreated regularly to the mausoleum to pray. With evident sincerity she anticipated her own life ending soon after that of her husband and commissioned from Marochetti a partner effigy for her own tomb. (In fact she survived her husband by so long that Marochetti's effigy was temporarily lost at the time of Victoria's death.) Throughout its evolution, the mausoleum absorbed her thoughts apparently more conspicuously than topics more generally considered within the sovereign's remit.

Such an assessment, which gained adherents throughout

the 1860s, told only part of the story, however. Victoria had seldom felt strongly about the finer points of domestic policy, although she was vigorous in defence of her constitutional rights in this as in all aspects of the working of government carried out in her name; over time she developed a lively interest in ecclesiastical appointments. Like Albert, she took a particular and personal interest in foreign policy; the first years of her widowhood were overshadowed by the warring claims of the Prussian and Danish crowns and the Duke of Augustenburg to the Duchies of Schleswig and Holstein. Although Albert had an eye for policy and an instinct for how best to advance the Crown's cause, Victoria, less sure of herself politically, was conscientious in the matter of paperwork. At her desk at Windsor, Osborne and Balmoral, she kept pace with the documentation of public life. It was not an undertaking from which she derived any satisfaction. To Leopold she described the impact of her work: 'constant anxiety, responsibility, and interruptions of every kind, where at every turn the heart is crushed and the wound is probed!'[24] This being the case, she *could* not understand any suggestion that the fulfilment of this clerical aspect of her position was not in itself enough. It was the bread and circuses of monarchy she shunned; it was for bread and circuses that the people increasingly bayed. In 1864, a notice outside Buckingham Palace announced: 'These commanding premises to be let or sold in consequence of the late occupant's declining business.' Something serious underpinned the ribaldry. Waspishly, author and journalist Margaret Oliphant, herself a widow supporting a family of young children, wrote to her publisher about Victoria's protracted retirement: 'A woman is surely a poor creature if with a large happy affectionate family of children around her, she can't take heart to do her duty whether she likes it or not.'[25] Victoria would have been stung by that argument – and intensely angry at its suggestion of duty neglected. That she felt able to censure the recently exiled Isabella II of Spain for 'misgovernment' indicates the extent to which she regarded herself as beyond such criticism.[26]

Quarter of a century ago, Leopold had warned her, 'Unfortunately, high personages are a little like stage actors – they must make efforts to please their public.'[27] Victoria was no longer the malleable girl of 1836 in thrall to her uncle's wisdom. For five years she resisted opening Parliament. She did so in 1866 only to ensure the safe passage of the grant of an annuity to her third daughter Helena, called 'Lenchen'. Victoria had recently engaged Lenchen to a balding and penniless princeling, Christian of Schleswig-Holstein-Sonderburg-Augustenburg. It was a cynical contract, her means of ensuring that Helena did not leave her but remained on hand to offer the support the grieving Queen regarded as essential from a grown-up daughter: 'Lenchen is so useful . . . that I could *not* give her up without *sinking* under the *weight* of my desolation.'[28] Amiable and undemonstrative, Christian was a man whose chief distinction lay in the euphoniousness of his empty title and his imperturbably equable disposition; Victoria jibbed at the condition of his teeth and dissipated his energies with the award of meaningless sinecures.

Despite her selfish motives, she regarded the process of opening Parliament that year as a cruel affront and the public desire to see her as 'unreasonable and unfeeling'. Expressing herself with characteristic forcefulness to Lord Russell, she cast herself in the light of a sacrificial victim: 'a poor, broken-hearted widow, nervous and shrinking, dragged in deep mourning, alone in State as a Show, where she used to go supported by her husband, to be gazed at, without delicacy of feeling'.[29] For five years she had withdrawn from public life, only occasionally venturing into the open to unveil or applaud some new memorial to Albert; once, in 1864, she travelled across London in an open carriage. She had forsaken the theatre, previously one of her chiefest pleasures, in the spring of 1861 during mourning for the Duchess of Kent, and determined never again to visit a London playhouse. Instead, as she discovered, she had herself become the spectacle: she would not accede with grace. Hereafter she regarded the pageantry of monarchy with enduring mistrust and a sense of begrudging. Yet she was still, as she insisted, Queen of England.

The commemorative poem that Tennyson wrote after Albert's death took the form of an extended dedication to a new edition of his *Idylls of the King*, which Albert himself had told Tennyson he admired. In blank verse, the poet wrestled with the catastrophe. Dutifully he claimed, 'The shadow of his loss drew like eclipse/ Darkening the world.' No one living with Victoria after Albert's death would have challenged that verdict. Victoria referred to 'this dead home';[30] it was she, not Albert, who made it so. She had transformed the Blue Room at Windsor Castle into a secular shrine. Across the bed, flowers were strewn like wishes; water for shaving, clean clothes and ink for Albert's pen were replenished daily. As with that blood-stained chair in which Frederick the Great had died and the glass case containing Victoire de Nemours's hair, inanimate objects served as relics in the cult, memory made tangible. Too late Tennyson proffered tactful advice in the form of a quotation from *Henry V*: 'O hard condition! Twin-born with greatness . . ./ What infinite heart's-ease must Kings neglect/ Which private men enjoy!'[31]

To the Queen of Prussia, Victoria wrote, 'My Angel was always so good and affectionate to his children, and always wanted them to be gay and happy.'[32] With Albert dead, Victoria omitted to prioritise her children's happiness. Alice criticised Helena's marriage to Christian as tending more to Victoria's wellbeing than Helena's. The haemophiliac Leopold found himself locked in a battle of wills with a mother determined to view him as an angelic invalid yearning for death, too unspoiled for this world of torments and sin; instead he craved university and afterwards marriage. For Louise and Beatrice, the youngest of the daughters, there would be little gaiety at home: for a period, even laughter was forbidden, every pleasure contraband. Only Arthur, the favourite son, experienced affection that was recognisably maternal. Dominating Victoria's relationships with all her children was that rivalry between the mother's and the sovereign's claims which she did not resolve. Her first thoughts were of herself, her requirements attentiveness and obedience. She had forgotten the unhappy years in Kensington; her loneliness, bereft of a father and companions of her own age; the daily impact of her painfully fissured relationship with her mother. She expected those children still young enough to live with her to enter fully into her suffering and otherwise to take comfort from the presence of their brothers and sisters; their older siblings she expected to support her in the insupportable burdens of her sadness and her work, 'the hard, ungrateful task I have to go through'.[33] 'The Queen . . . never appears so queenly, so true a woman, as when surrounded by her children,' wrote John Darton with unwitting irony in 1864, in *Famous Girls Who Have Become Illustrious Women*.[34] For the children in question physical proximity to their mother was not enough, nor her queenliness, not even her womanliness.

'How should England dreaming of his sons/ Hope more for these than some inheritance/ Of such a life, a heart, a mind as thine,/ Thou noble Father of her Kings to be,' asked Tennyson. Albert's sons, like his daughters, hoped for more. For questions she refused to hear, Victoria had no answers.

8

'A Highland Widow'

IN THE WINTER of 1863, Victoria labelled a new photograph in her personal album 'A Highland Widow'. The image was of herself, taken at Balmoral by George Washington Wilson on 20 October. She was mounted on a black pony called Fyvie. She was dressed entirely in black, her custom now, reins held loosely in gloved hands, eyes downcast, apparently unseeing. At the pony's head, steadily outfacing the camera, stood John Brown.

Since 1858, John Brown had served as Victoria's personal servant in Scotland, handy, surefooted and reassuring, as she thought him. He combined in one person 'the offices of groom, footman, page and *maid*'.[1] That comprehensive remit was guaranteed to appeal to Victoria, with her need to be the exclusive object of the ministrations of those nearest to her; in that respect she did not distinguish between servants, courtiers or her family. An empiricist in personal relationships, she demanded proof of devotion in the form of wholehearted absorption in her own concerns. Brown had been engaged by Albert in 1851, before the building of the new castle, when the couple's Highland home retained the romance of a dream; he was subsequently promoted to the role of Victoria's 'particular ghillie'. Maid of honour Eleanor Stanley, encountering him as such in 1854, apostrophised 'the most fascinating and good-looking young Highlander, John Brown'.[2] Albert's choice could not be wrong. The *Aberdeen Herald & Weekly Free Press* later explained his initial recommendation as 'his magnificent physique, his transparent honesty and straightforward, independent character'.[3] Honesty and independence of character were also part of Victoria's makeup; as her life-changing response to Albert's appearance on a staircase at Windsor Castle in 1839 proved, she too was susceptible to a magnificent physique.

By 1863, like Victoria herself, Brown had become a relic of Albert's Balmoral. In this he was doubly blessed for Victoria: associated with her 'beloved Angel' as well as with the 'dear Paradise' which husband and wife had hewn from glittering Aberdeenshire granite more than six hours from London. Albert's death might easily have spelled a tailing off of Brown's royal service. Instead, in the autumn of 1864, he travelled from Deeside to the Isle of Wight.

The idea was not Victoria's. It amounted to little less than a plot, its conspirators Dr Jenner, Clark's replacement as Personal Physician, and Sir Charles Phipps, Keeper of the Privy Purse. Adept in their mistress's ways, they consulted Victoria before setting the plot in motion, making her a co-conspirator to her own reawakening at the hands of this burly *deus ex machina*. Their purpose was to rekindle Victoria's interest in riding, and they correctly estimated that a familiar face would succeed where newer grooms were likely to fail. As Victoria commented complacently, 'I am weak & nervous, & very dependent on those I am accustomed to.'[4]

Jenner and Phipps did not anticipate the rapid expansion of Brown's sphere of activity. His usefulness to Victoria was soon more than that of coachman or groom. In February 1865, she wrote to Leopold of Brown's promotion to attend her '*always* and everywhere out of doors, whether riding or driving or on foot; and it is a *real* comfort, for he is *so* devoted to me – so simple, so intelligent, so unlike an *ordinary* servant, and so cheerful and attentive'.[5] He was appointed 'The Queen's Highland Servant', at a salary of £120 a year. On 1 March, signalling the way the wind was blowing, Victoria informed her eldest daughter that Brown's 'observations upon everything he sees and hears are excellent and many show how superior in feeling, sense and judgement he is to the servants here!'[6] She quoted an example of his homespun philosophy.

Once Victoria had valued the Highlands for their 'retirement', their 'wildness', 'liberty' and 'solitude', a romantic and picturesque landscape of innate superiority, which, like the landscape of poetry and novels, thrilled on an imaginative as well as a visual level. The constant presence of John Brown encouraged a similar conviction of the superiority of Highlanders themselves, their unspoiled outlook untamed by the courtier's moues and blandishments, free from cant and the oiliness of place-seeking. It was not what Jenner and Phipps had intended, although the quickening of the royal pulse, whatever its source, represented progress of a sort. In 1864, Victoria's half-sister Feodore had cut short a visit intended to last four months. 'I have not the moral strength to see you and hear you so constantly unhappy,' she had offered by way of explanation.[7] A year later, by contrast, Victoria not only countenanced a resumption of those theatricals the royal children had formerly staged at Osborne, but herself attended a rehearsal in the Council Room. In her journal, she reserved her commendations for her favourite son, fourteen-year-old Arthur.

With Brown a permanent fixture, Victoria's life surrendered that wholly sedentary character it had assumed after Albert's death. To carriage drives was added suitably sedate riding; in the Highlands there were picnics and even excursions on foot. The kilted Highlander, rugged in appearance and expression, was always to hand. Given Victoria's inability to live entirely in the moment, there were inevitably photographs to transform the troubling present into the black-and-white safety of the past. There were more photographs like Victoria's 'A Highland Widow'. And then in 1867, a painting unlike any other which preceded it, an attempt to unite in a single image Victoria's roles of grieving widow and abandoned mother, and royal bureaucrat. The painting in question depicts black-clad Victoria on a stationary black pony, the artist tactful in the matter of his sitter's expanding girth. Again John Brown, suitably funereal in black kilt and stockings, holds the pony's head. Brown stares at the pony; Victoria, with a suggestion of a frown, reads a letter. In the background Osborne House, lumpen above broad terraces. At the pony's feet, Victoria's discarded gloves, a confetti of letters and envelopes, a dispatch box, two dogs. Studies in lassitude, Princesses Helena and Louise occupy a nearby bench. It is a striking and peculiar painting. Its questionable success lies in its portrayal of a startling if unsettling intimacy between rider and ghillie.

In her journal, Victoria recorded her intention that the picture present her 'as I am now, sad & lonely, seated on my pony, led by Brown, with a representation of Osborne'.[8] In his London studio, her chosen artist, Edwin Landseer (since 1850 Sir Edwin) worked from photographs, requesting assistance with the faulty view of the house and blaming the city's blanket-like fogs for his slow progress. Hypochondriac, tormented by demons, suffering with his eyes, nervous, depressed and hard-drinking, he struggled to complete on time what he called 'the Widow's Picture'. It would be displayed with the innocuous title *Her Majesty at Osborne in 1866*. Landseer claimed for it the distinction of conveying, as Victoria intended, a *'truthful and unaffected* representation of Her Majesty's unceasing grief',[9] as once upon a time his paintings had celebrated her joy. But neither Victoria's intentions nor Landseer's assertions – not even its noncommittal title – could safeguard the fate of what became the most controversial painting Victoria commissioned: on public view at the Royal Academy in May 1867, it caused a sensation.

Contemporary audiences with a taste for narrative painting, accustomed to 'reading' and forensically decoding such images, interpreted Landseer's vignette of work-oppressed grief in quite a different light. Correctly they dismissed the curious artifice of Victoria's equine workstation ringed by fallen papers. They were not distracted by the predictable charm of the begging terrier. Overlooked were the figures of Helena and Louise, modest chaperones. 'All is black that is not Brown,' quipped a new satirical weekly. For the public gazed . . . and the public saw. And what they saw appeared to amount to confirmation from Victoria herself of a rumour which explained more convincingly than grief the reason for her malingering absences from London. Here was the truth of her widow's life in the Isle of Wight and the Highlands, away from prying eyes. In 1863, Victoria had explained, 'It is not the Queen's *sorrow* that keeps her secluded . . . it is her *overwhelming work* and her health.'[10] Landseer's painting suggested alternative motives for Victoria's withdrawal from public view; it suggested a dilettantish quality to her work; in the stoutness of her figure it suggested the return of health.

Although Victoria herself was pleased with the painting, promptly entrusting Landseer with a commission to engrave it and a fresh dispatch of photographs recording Brown's new shorter beard to ensure maximum accuracy, she could hardly have judged popular feeling less adroitly. As *The Saturday Review* commented with some asperity, 'If anyone will stand by this picture for a quarter of an hour and listen to the comments of visitors he will learn how great an imprudence has been committed.'[11] Even *The Illustrated London News* expressed disappointment: 'there is not one of Her Majesty's subjects will see this lugubrious picture without regret'.[12] The following year, an American visitor to London claimed in *Tinsley's Magazine* that he had been shocked by 'constant references to and jokes about "Mrs Brown" . . . an English synonym for the Queen . . .'[13] It was a joke which had been current in court circles for some time. In June 1865, at Windsor Castle, Lord Stanley had expressed his reservations at Victoria distinguishing Brown 'beyond what is customary or fitting in [his] position', treatment which had earned her the nickname 'Mrs Brown'. 'If it lasts,' Stanley warned, 'the joke will grow into a scandal.'[14] So it would prove.

Once, in the dark days after December 1861, Victoria had shed tears for the loss of the physical aspect of Albert's love. 'I am, alas! not old, and my feelings are strong and warm; my love is ardent,' she had protested.[15] The romantic flutterings of her youth – that girlish heart set aquiver by the Tsarevitch or the exiled Duke of Brunswick – had found fuller satisfaction in her marriage to Albert. Understandably Victoria's lament encompassed more than the withdrawal of what she labelled Albert's 'finer feelings'. That she satisfied this shortfall after an interval with a square-jawed, sturdy-limbed Highland servant so devoted to her that in eighteen years he did not take a single day's holiday from his continual duties is an evergreen rumour. No evidence supports it, bar those testimonies she herself left to her affection for John Brown: in her letters and her journal, in those memorials she created to him in print and solider matter. She called him 'darling one'; '. . . so often I told him no one loved him more than I did or had a better friend than me: and he answered "Nor you – than me . . . No one loves you more."'[16] She gave him Valentine's Day cards of cloying winsomeness. The very artlessness of such tokens – incriminating to modern ears – are proof of Victoria's innocence, this woman whose candour and iron truthfulness so often expose her meagreness and folly.

In the beginning John Brown was another servant, although he consistently found particular favour following his journey south. In letters to Vicky during the spring of 1865, Victoria referred to him as 'J. Brown', an address lacking in intimacy. She praised him as 'one in a thousand' on account of his 'unflinching straightforwardness and honesty; great moral courage; unselfishness and rare discretion and devotion',[17] and thus forged a bond between them for these were in part her own virtues. To her daughter she expressed without dissimulation her pleasure in the 'excellent arrangement' of her affairs since Brown had taken on the role of maid-of-all-work. But she explained that role with reference to other servants, no suggestion that Brown had stepped outside his allotted sphere. The key to the ghillie's success was his willingness to focus exclusively on Victoria: it provided grounds for what became her unshakeable conviction of Highlanders' loyalty.

'I feel I have here and always in the house a good devoted soul,' she wrote to Vicky on 5 April 1865, 'whose only object and interest is my service, and God knows how I want so much to be taken care of.'[18] Initially Vicky congratulated her mother on an arrangement that suited her so admirably. Three years later, as Victoria prepared for a holiday in Switzerland, Brown's inclusion in the party arose partly at Vicky's suggestion.[19] Brown himself loathed the experience of being abroad. His fondness for the country would not have been increased by an article published in the *Gazette de Lausanne* in September 1866. The paper's anonymous correspondent claimed that a pregnant Victoria had been forced to cancel engagements. The child's father was John Brown, the couple having previously contracted a morganatic marriage. Victoria would have been forty-seven at the time. John Brown was seven years her junior.

Victoria's future private secretary Henry Ponsonby stated matter-of-factly that Brown was conspicuous on account of his Highland dress: riding on the box of Victoria's carriage during her few public engagements, he presented a distinctive figure. The distinctive treatment Victoria accorded her Highland servant, however, took place within royal precincts, out of sight of a curious public. She consistently singled him out from her other servants, her courtiers and her children too. Brown received his orders direct from Victoria: he attended her in her room after breakfast for that purpose and was understood to come and go without knocking, as once Lehzen had done.

In a remarkably short space of time, Brown had become indispensable to Victoria: rather than communicating directly with her equerries, she did so through Brown, in Victoria's mind a conduit, too often a barrier between Queen and court. There were rumours too that he spied on Victoria's behalf. His unambiguous loyalty qualified him for a position of trust; the abrasiveness of his manner and his temper, his laconic brusqueness and granite-hard insolence, seemed to jeer at the perpetually ruffled feathers of Victoria's hothouse court. Too many of those in waiting roundly detested Balmoral; Brown's lordly ubiquity redoubled that disaffection. Accommodation was cramped and icy, Victoria stubbornly convinced of the health-giving properties of cold air; the weather was joyless and the atmosphere one of unrelenting tedium as Victoria sat spinning Aberdeenshire flax at her spinning wheel and listening to the poetry of Robert Burns; members of the household were circumscribed even in smoking. In addition, the greater degree of informality Victoria embraced in her Highland holiday home eroded those finer distinctions of hierarchy by which members of the household set store. The below stairs world became a Brown suzerainty with the employment of several of John Brown's brothers. Their regime lacked kindliness – even towards Victoria's family. Off duty, Brown drank to excess. Courtiers seethed. Impotently, Victoria's children nurtured mounting grievances. It was Victoria's own attendants who first dubbed her Brown's wife, a calumny born of spite or possibly amusement. Perhaps they meant to shame her into a separation.[20] They were no match for Victoria's obduracy and misguided to attempt coercion by force: their efforts failed. With less hope of victory, the princesses dismissed Brown airily as 'mama's lover'.

Six years after Landseer's death, Victoria called on painter Charles Burton Barber to make a second version of *Her Majesty at Osborne in 1866*. The later painting reproduces the first composition with significant differences. Osborne is replaced by Balmoral and a backdrop less manicured; gone are signs of Victoria's occupation and the decorative chaperonage of her daughters. Instead, in this second image, which Victoria gave to John Brown as a present in 1876, the same year she gave him a cottage at Balmoral, nothing detracts from the focus on the drama's chief protagonists. In *Queen Victoria seated on 'Florrie', John Brown in Attendance, Balmoral in the Distance*, Brown stares fixedly at the pony's face. Victoria stares at Brown. It is a pregnant moment.

By 1876, for Victoria's contemporaries, the scandal of 'Mrs Brown' was past. Victoria herself had done nothing to address it. Rather her slow return to royal duties and her increasing visibility, with Brown invariably in attendance in public, denied grounds for suspicion of a liaison that was evidently neither clandestine nor furtive. In 1867, for the first time, Victoria had been provided with the services of a private secretary, the affable but not entirely sympathetic General Charles Grey; in 1870, he was succeeded by the better-suited Henry Ponsonby: wry, astute, of superhuman tact and unflagging patience, politically moderate and respectful without sycophancy. The presence of both men lessened some of Victoria's reliance on John Brown. Victoria understood the nature of the tittle-tattle that briefly came close to undermining her: with some justification she attributed it to '*ill-natured gossip in the higher classes*'. In the summer of 1867, when feelings ran high following display of Landseer's painting, she had confronted that ill-natured gossip. She had refused to attend a military review in Hyde Park without John Brown's 'strong arm' to support her, despite the Prime Minister, Lord Derby, warning her that demonstrations were planned against Brown. Victoria smelled a rat: a bully herself, she understood when she was being bullied. She expressed herself 'much astonished and shocked' at the attempts to manipulate her and frighten her into leaving Brown at home. Monarch and ministers swiftly reached an impasse, which was broken only by the death by shooting squad of the Emperor of Mexico, a royal cousin by marriage. A grateful government cancelled the review. Victoria reverted to default mode, reiterating her mantra, 'The Queen will not be dictated to'. As in her dealings with Sir Robert Peel over the Bedchamber Crisis, she appeared to have carried the day; victory by intransigence.

Before John Brown's death on 27 March 1883, Victoria increased his salary on at least three occasions. She formally designated him 'Esquire'. In letters from mistress to servant, she signed herself 'your faithful friend', confident that her friendship was returned.[21] She was not mistaken. It was, in fact, the principal service John Brown had rendered Victoria. Unwittingly he had encouraged her in a course of escapism that tarnished her popularity and significantly damaged the monarchy. At her death, his photograph was placed inside her coffin, held within the stiff, unbending fingers of her left hand.

9

'Wisest counsellors'

'ONE OF THE kindest, truest and best friends and wisest counsellors she ever had', re-entered Victoria's life in the 1860s. His florid chivalry and sumptuous flattery mitigated any sneering behind the cordons of the Royal Academy or in scurrilous weekly papers, and obliterated those uncertain first impressions Victoria had formed of him two decades earlier as an opponent of Peel. His name was Benjamin Disraeli. From 1866 he served as Chancellor of the Exchequer in Lord Derby's Tory government. In February 1868, following the passing of a second Reform Act, which Victoria approved, and Derby's retirement through gout, which she also approved, Disraeli became prime minister. He served for a mere nine months before losing the general election to Gladstone's Liberals, but returned in 1874, aged seventy, for a second term. Famously he referred to Victoria as 'the Faery'. He likened her to the fairy queen Titania, her realm a bower – notwithstanding her portliness and the high colour she derived from overeating, wilfulness, nervous apprehension and excessively cold rooms. The suggestion of magic in these dainty gallantries was his not hers.

Never had magic been more necessary than as Victoria

entered her fifties. Of the State Opening of Parliament in December 1857, Lady Charlotte Schreiber had written: 'The Queen was received with very little enthusiasm, and . . . it was a flat affair.'[1] A decade of sorrowful concealment had further diminished popular enthusiasm for the lachrymose monarch. She had failed to respond to every call to resume her former life of pomp and ceremony. In 1865, *Punch* published a cartoon inspired by *The Winter's Tale*. It reimagined the moment of Hermione's magical reawakening from statue to living flesh in Act 5. In the cartoon Victoria takes on the role of Hermione, turned to stone, Britannia upbraiding her: 'Tis time! Descend! Be stone no more!' All in vain. Victoria had begun to depend on her seclusion as proof of her continuing fidelity to Albert's memory; the masquerade of grief absolved her from distasteful exertions. Instead, in 1868, she found an alternative means of displaying herself to public view.

Against the wishes of her children, she published *Leaves from the Journal of Our Life in the Highlands*. A selection of diary extracts from 1842 to 1868, carefully edited to convey an impression of wholesome if unceasing royal leisure at Balmoral, the book earned Victoria fulsome plaudits in the popular press and impressive sales figures (*Leaves* outsold, for example, Wilkie Collins's *The Moonstone* and Robert Browning's *The Ring and the Book*, both also published in 1868). In addition, as *The Times* averred, it permitted her subjects to be 'the sharers in her own personal joys and sorrows', a policy which would ultimately reap dividends in re-cementing Crown and country.[2] Its runaway success delighted Victoria. Disingenuously she wrote to Theodore Martin on 16 January, 'What has she done to be so loved & liked?', a more pertinent question than she apparently realised and one that Martin quailed to address directly.[3] At the same time, among a vocal minority, publication stimulated criticism of an otiose existence of picnics, sketching and flannel petticoats for cottagers that offered the nation a poor return on the annual Civil List payment of £385,000: *Leaves* forcibly drew attention to precisely those aspects of Victoria's behaviour which served to weaken the bond between sovereign and people. It reiterated her widow's grief, dedicated 'to the dear memory of him who made the life of the writer bright and happy', and was thickly larded with references to Highland servants. Conspicuous among the latter was John Brown. A typical entry, for 18 September 1858, depicts Brown helping to carry Victoria through wet grass, borne aloft on his shoulders. Such insights confirmed the misgivings of Victoria's detractors, further swelling ranks which were already worryingly bloated. From Berlin, Vicky observed with concern that the dangers of republicanism were 'daily spreading'.

With what she regarded as his 'poetry, romance and chivalry' – though an eye to the preservation of the status quo might be a nearer explanation – Disraeli had taken pains throughout his fleeting premiership to reignite Victoria's awareness of her place in the political system. He cultivated an appearance of relying on her assistance with the great affairs of state. Lengthily he wrote to her, employing to the full those gifts which had made him a bestselling novelist. Smilingly he insisted that 'all his own thoughts and feelings and duties and affections are now concentrated in your Majesty',[4] and outlined 'every scrap of political news dressed up to serve his own purpose, and every scrap of social gossip cooked to amuse her'. His cynicism hit its target. Victoria 'declare[d] that she ha[d] never had *such* letters in her life . . . and that she never before knew *everything*!'[5] Given that the overwhelming interest to Victoria of Disraeli's first ministry was a series of Church appointments, matters debated behind closed doors, and the future of the Irish Church, the assiduous conjurer nonetheless failed to lure his Faery out of her hidden bowers back into the public gaze. In 1868, Gladstone, lacking Disraeli's black arts, inherited a queen still set on a course of determined seclusion and a population, *Leaves* or no *Leaves*, no longer over-sympathetic to her perpetual woes.

But Gladstone was a man of conviction and resolve. In the time he could spare from the equally thorny business of pacifying Ireland, he set about ending Victoria's retirement. In neither aim did he meet with notable success. That year, Victoria built her 'Widow's House', the Glassalt Shiel. Two and a half miles from Balmoral, in an isolated clearing thick with midges, it was 'a silent place, the quietness only broken by the trickle of a waterfall high above and the cries of water birds'.[6] She described it as 'the only place in the world where I can have complete rest'.[7] Four-square and, to outsiders, cheerless, it expressed in concrete form Victoria's continuing reclusiveness. At Brown's suggestion she even smoked to keep the midges at bay. Its very inaccessibility kept all else at bay.

With an ill grace, Victoria agreed to open Joseph Cubbit's new Blackfriars Bridge, a Venetian Gothic fantasy of granite and colourfully painted wrought iron, on 6 November 1869, attended by a mounted escort and the full panoply of royal parade; she insisted her compliance 'must NEVER be made a *precedent*' and again declined to open Parliament. Bertie added his entreaties to those of the Prime Minister, with predictable results. 'We live in radical times,' he told his mother, 'and [the] more the people see the Sovereign, the better it is for the *people* and the *country*.'[8] As ever, Victoria's response to confrontation was unreasoning rebuttal. Her growing conviction that

Gladstone meant to harry her into acting against her wishes served to harden her implacability and soured relations with a prime minister to whom she was at first tolerably well disposed. By the autumn of 1869 she was writing to Vicky, 'I cannot find him very agreeable.'[9] Although Albert had once approved of Gladstone's high-mindedness and religiosity, Victoria would ultimately loathe him. He was wordy, conscientious and theoretical. She refused to admire his idealism, with its challenge to her own petty selfishness. Eventually she dismissed him as a lunatic, 'that half-mad firebrand'.[10] She suspected him of inclining towards dictatorship, while John Brown encouraged further wariness on religious grounds: Gladstone's High Church zeal offended the anti-Catholicism of mistress and ghillie. Disraeli was theatrical. About Gladstone, preoccupied in his own words with 'candle-ends and cheese-parings', hung a whiff of the mercantile trade (grain and sugar) on which his family's fortune was based – as Disraeli dismissed him aphoristically, 'preaching, praying, speechifying or scribbling, never a gentleman'. To Disraeli, Victoria dispatched boxes of primroses from Windsor, acknowledging his status as ageing cavalier, with his black-dyed ringlets and perfumed compliments. She sent him a collection of Albert's speeches, bound and inscribed, and in time Koberwein's copy of her most formidable portrait, by Heinrich von Angeli, tactfully described by Vicky as 'a trifle stern and set';[11] it hung in the 'Gallery of Affection' at his house in Buckinghamshire. Despite his wife's encouragement, Gladstone could not, like his opponent, 'pet the Queen'. And so he failed to convince her of the depths of his reverence for the institution she embodied and his personal determination to safeguard her position.

By the beginning of the 1870s that position was more precarious than it had ever been. Support for republicanism, arguably never a serious threat, nevertheless scaled new levels and inspired widespread misgivings. Victoria continued to assert with customary vehemence that she had 'failed in none of her regal duties. It is abominable that a woman and a Queen laden with care and with public and domestic anxieties which are daily increasing should not be able to make people understand that there is a limit to her powers.'[12] But people were indeed unable to understand. For many of her subjects, Victoria's absenteeism downgraded her to queen in name alone. The Prince of Wales, by contrast, was all too prominent: 'no one looks up to him, though all like him', Victoria surmised.[13] In 1870, Bertie found himself conspicuously embroiled in a society divorce case which dissipated much of that liking. Letters from Bertie to the errant wife, Lady Mordaunt, were read out in court. The letters themselves were notable for their blandness, and the behaviour of Harriett Mordaunt indicated mental derangement, but the damaging effect on Bertie's reputation of such unlovely associations was considerable. It was against this background that Victoria agreed to open Parliament. It was noted, however, that her willingness coincided with the engagement of her fourth daughter Louise to the Marquess of Lorne and Arthur's attainment of his majority, both events she intended to be marked by her government with financial settlements. This final suggestion of calculating avarice prompted publication of the anonymous pamphlet, *What Does She Do With It?*, which provided a rallying point for Victoria's critics.

The author, Liberal MP George Trevelyan, argued that, in abandoning the pageantry of monarchy, Victoria was hoarding up to £200,000 of public money every year, exploiting her widowhood and constant nervous indisposition to set aside hefty profits for the Privy Purse. Newspapers took up the cry. When Victoria, claiming illness, departed for Balmoral before the end of the Parliamentary session, her behaviour – self-indulgent and petulantly uncooperative as it appeared – prompted a full-scale witch-hunt.

She had cried wolf once too often. Ironically, in this instance, Victoria *was* ill. On 22 August 1871, she wrote, 'Never since I was a girl, when I had typhoid fever at Ramsgate in '35, have I felt so ill.'[14] After a throat infection, she developed an abscess on her arm six inches in diameter; it was followed by a severe attack of gout and rheumatoid arthritis. She lost the use of her legs and was forced to use a wheeled chair, John Brown the only person strong enough to lift her in and out of the chair and even in and out of bed. Such was the pain in her arm that she dictated her journal to her youngest daughter. Gladstone had condemned her refusal not to alter the date of her departure for the Highlands – 'smaller and meaner causes for the decay of Thrones cannot be conceived';[15] afterwards he relented. So, too, Victoria's children, who had planned jointly to send their mother a letter, written by Vicky, imploring Victoria to end her seclusion and banish the spectre of revolution. The letter was never sent. *The Times* apologised for its erstwhile scepticism, while *The Daily News* drew a picture of a nation chastened and ashamed.[16] It was not enough.

On 6 November 1871, while Victoria convalesced at Balmoral, a youthful MP called Sir Charles Wentworth Dilke addressed a meeting of working men in Newcastle. His subject was the need for an alternative to the monarchy in the face of Victoria's dereliction of duty, and Dilke's audience applauded him heartily. 'There is a widespread belief that a Republic here is only a matter of education and time,' he stated. 'If you can show me a fair chance that a Republic here will be free from the political corruption that hangs about the Monarchy, I say, for my part . . . let it come.'[17] From her sickbed Victoria roused herself to respond with fury. Gladstone, who regarded republicanism as 'a distemper', attempted to soothe her with assurances that he considered the matter one of 'grave public importance'.[18]

Ten years had passed since Albert's death. In 1863, Stockmar had also died, followed two years later by Victoria's uncle Leopold. Jointly the three men had conceived of the reform of Britain's throne, an overhaul in the wake of late-Georgian folly. Victoria was queen in a new mould, service and duty her watchwords, her court exemplary for its moral probity. Victoria's Britain had resisted revolution in 1848, the year of European convulsions. Even the collapse of the Second Empire in France and the exile to an ugly house at Chislehurst of Napoleon III and his lovely Empress Eugénie had not toppled Victoria's throne. But the clamour was rising. In Hyde Park, a republican rally attracted large crowds. Parliament's vote of a dowry of £30,000 to Princess Louise provoked boisterous criticism at public meetings in Nottingham and Birmingham. The *Pall Mall Gazette* reported 'republicanism of a very revolutionary form flooding in'.[19] All at a moment when Victoria was too weak to defend herself against such slings and arrows. Salvation came from the one quarter she would never have countenanced: her eldest son, Bertie.

On 22 November 1871, Victoria's journal records: 'Breakfasted for the first time again with my children, and I felt it was a step forward and I was returning to ordinary life.' Her tone of relief proved short-lived. She went on to confirm that she been informed that 'dear Bertie had "mild typhoid fever"'. Unsurprisingly this typhoid widow described her reaction as one of anxiety.[20]

After a week's grouse-shooting with Lord and Lady Londesborough at a house party near Scarborough distinguished by the unusually high incidence of diarrhoea, Bertie had returned to Sandringham for his thirtieth birthday. There he and Alix were joined by his sister Alice. His complaints of feeling unwell resulted in a prompt diagnosis. Fresh from administering to Victoria at Balmoral, Alice resumed her recurrent task of nursing. She summoned a royal doctor, William Gull, in place of the local Norfolk practitioner. Reports issued at once to members of the press charted the textbook progression of Bertie's illness. Within a short space its seemingly relentless advance led from optimism to deepest pessimism.

The effect on the public of this unexpected and sombre drama was electric. Bertie's illness gripped the nation. Signs of recovery on 1 December were followed within less than a week by a recrudescence sufficiently alarming to warrant four-hourly bulletins to the press. As the fever entered its third week, Victoria reported receipt of 'no end of recommendations of remedies of the most mad kind' from concerned members of the public whose letters and telegrams arrived like a deluge.[21] Victoria installed herself at Sandringham, a house she had never previously visited although it was Albert who had negotiated its purchase at the bargain price of £220,000; with her were her children and even peripheral members of the royal family, including the former George of Cambridge, now Duke of Cambridge. What comfort Victoria provided either Bertie or Alix is questionable: her thoughts were inevitably of death. 'How all reminded me so vividly and sadly of my dearest Albert's illness,' she sighed.[22] While Victoria ordered domestic arrangements to suit herself, even in the midst of crisis and regardless of the inconvenience to Alix, watchers across the country awaited the latest development. For Victoria was not alone in remembering Albert's last weeks. Almost miraculously, Bertie's misfortune had brought about a reconciliation between sovereign and subjects, a widespread expression of sympathy which *The Graphic* hailed as 'a satisfactory proof of the loyalty of the nation'.[23] For three days Bertie's life hung in the balance. Not only Victoria but all those at Sandringham, as well as journalists, clergymen and Gladstone, despaired of his recovery. Gull described him as 'on the very *verge* of the grave', adding that 'hardly anyone has recovered who has been *so* ill'.[24] 'The worst day of all' was Wednesday 13 December, the eve of the tenth anniversary of Albert's death, when every hope faded. Unnecessarily, as it happened, for on 14 December, Bertie rounded the corner.

In the weeks that followed, with Alix's eager support and characteristic curmudgeonliness on Victoria's part, Gladstone made plans for a national service of thanksgiving. That celebration, at St Paul's Cathedral on 27 February 1872 – a state occasion at the Prime Minister's insistence – completed the overthrow of the republican animosity Victoria had brought upon herself. Myriad well-wishers packed the bunting-strung streets of the capital; 'every window was thronged, every tree, lamp-post, and paling were used as perches, and what was really singular was the way in which the sloping London roofs were somehow converted into standing places . . .'[25] Later Victoria described it as 'a day that can never be forgotten'.[26] She had played her part well, dressed in fur-trimmed silk, afterwards acknowledging the cheering crowds from the balcony of Buckingham Palace. Moved by the warmth of her reception, she had displayed an instinct for showmanship otherwise confined to her

portraiture, responding to rapturous cheering at Temple
Bar by raising Bertie's hand in her own and kissing it. A
relieved Gladstone described Londoners' beneficence
simply and truthfully as 'a quite extraordinary manifestation of loyalty and affection'. A subsequent request by
Dilke that the House of Commons investigate the royal
finances met with raucous derision, an ignominious end
to a reasonable crusade. Victoria knighted Dr Gull.
Whether or not she acknowledged it as such, it
represented her thanks for more than illness cured.

'I am an Empress and in common conversation am
sometimes called Empress of India. Why have I never
officially assumed this title? I feel I ought to do so and
wish to have preliminary enquiries made,' Victoria wrote
to Ponsonby on 27 January 1873.[27] The idea was one of
long gestation. Twenty years earlier, in receipt of
spectacular jewels from the Treasury of Lahore, Victoria
had commissioned from the Crown Jewellers Garrard &
Co. 'Oriental' jewellery, including a tiara of 'Moghul' arches
framing opal-studded diamond lotus flowers; in 1861,
under Albert's guidance, she instituted the Order of the
Star of India and held the Order's first investiture on what
she referred to as 'the second anniversary of my assumption
of the Government of India'.[28] In all her dealings with the
subcontinent, Victoria would retain this personal and
possessive note. Enquiries having been set in motion in
1873, her resolve quickly grew. Ponsonby recorded her
'*determination*' to 'take the additional title of Empress of
India':[29] the words were Victoria's own. Ditto the buoyant
spirit of self-assertion, the lofty sense of station and the
romantic enthusiasm for an exotic and otherworldly realm
she would never visit but which in imagination she claimed
as her own particular fiefdom.

Formally conferred in 1876, the title was widely regarded as Disraeli's personal gift to the Queen; she in turn rewarded him with a peerage. A cartoon published in *Punch* on 15 April, 'New Crowns for Old Ones! (Aladdin Adapted)', depicted the Prime Minister in the guise of Abanazar offering Victoria a splendid new Indian coronet.[30] Nimbly Disraeli had encouraged the suggestion of magic in his relationship with his 'Faery'. Monarch and minister inhabited an enchanted realm in which, in keeping with his apothegm of never refusing, never contradicting and sometimes forgetting, everything was possible that tended to the happiness of the former. In 1875, for example, he announced the government's purchase of shares in the Suez Canal as a tribute to Victoria herself: 'It is just settled: you have it, Madam.' Inevitably the truth was often less halcyon. Opposition to the Royal Titles Act was vociferous. Associated with the thrones of Russia, Napoleonic France and, since 1871, the newly united Germany, imperial titles suggested to British ears absolutism and a tendency contrary to that spirit of political progress enshrined in two Reform Acts. The bill's tempestuous passage through Parliament, and hostile references to 'imperialism' in sections of the press – the *Daily Telegraph*, for example, demonised the Act as a 'sinister revolution'[31] – surprised and angered Victoria, who exclaimed against the 'disgraceful agitation' of the Opposition;[32] her conviction of public support for the measure and all it represented did not waver. Gladstone dismissed the title as 'theatrical bombast and folly'.[33]

If the bombast were Victoria's, the element of theatricality was Disraeli's and considered on his part. For Disraeli, Victoria's additional title asserted the personal rule of the Crown over the colony which had come under direct government control only in 1858, following suppression of the Indian Mutiny, and focused the loyalty of India's diverse population on the person of the sovereign. To an unconvinced Lord Salisbury, Secretary of State for India, he claimed, 'What may have been looked upon as an ebullition of personal vanity may bear the semblance of deep and organised policy.'[34] At Disraeli's suggestion, the new Viceroy of India, Lord Lytton, proclaimed Victoria's title with 'every possible éclat' on 1 January 1877, at a durbar of such magnificence that Valentine Prinsep's painting of the event took three years to complete and, at more than seven metres long, required the artist specially to enlarge his Holland Park studio in order to accommodate the canvas.[35] For her part, Victoria chose the simpler medium of photography to broadcast her elevation. She was photographed by W. & D. Downey on the ivory throne presented to her in 1850 by the Maharaja Marthanda Varma of Travancore. She wore a magnificent brooch set with the Koh-i-Noor diamond of the Maharajas of Lahore, which she had previously worn to sit for Winterhalter, and a suitably earnest expression all her own. Although her new title had been intended for use only in connection with imperial matters, from the outset Victoria signed herself VRI, *Victoria Regina et Imperatrix* (Queen and Empress). Fifteen years after Albert's death, she had disentangled herself from the entwined 'V' and 'A' of the dual cipher: the splendour was her own. As she had claimed for herself in 1874, she had become indeed '*Doyenne* of Sovereigns', gilded with the glitter and spoils of the Orient, secure on her increased throne: a reigning monarch, as she asserted, for almost twenty years longer than that bugbear of the Crimean, the Tsar of Russia. She was fifty-seven years old.

10

'Mother of many nations'

FROM DOWNING STREET, Disraeli, now Earl of Beaconsfield, wrote to congratulate Victoria on 13 May 1879 on the birth of her first great-grandchild, Princess Feodora of Saxe-Meiningen. 'Your Majesty has become the "mother of many nations" . . . May all, that now occurs, be for your happiness and glory!'[1] Victoria herself described the birth of the eldest child of the eldest daughter of her own eldest daughter more simply as 'quite an event'.[2]

That complacent assessment represented a shift in her thinking. A decade earlier, her response to the birth of Bertie and Alix's second daughter, Princess Victoria of Wales, had been disparaging. To Vicky she had written on 10 July 1868, 'I fear the seventh granddaughter and fourteenth grandchild becomes a very uninteresting thing – for it seems to me to go on like the rabbits in Windsor Park.'[3] Liberated at last from the chrysalis of her gloom, she now increasingly allowed her thoughts to move in channels of which Albert would have approved. On his twenty-first wedding anniversary Albert had described to Stockmar his marriage to Victoria as 'green and fresh, and [throwing] out vigorous roots, from which I can, with gratitude to God, acknowledge that much good will be engendered to the world'.[4] His grandiloquence embraced dynastic intent and a degree of idealism: hindsight mocks his hifalutin certainty. Above all, Albert had dreamed of peace. Those dreams outstripped his own lifespan and also that of his widow; within years of her death all would be shattered. But in her final decades she, who had preferred introspection and withdrawal, again looked outwards. Disraeli had encouraged in Victoria a reappraisal of the possibilities of her position. Giddy with his compliments, exhilarated by her imperial vocation and confident, since 1872, of popular acclaim, she conceived a new role for herself, appropriate in grandeur and extent: 'mother of many nations', as Disraeli acclaimed her. To that would be added the homelier epithet of 'Grandmama of Europe'. This femininised domain suggested a family of nations both imperial and European. Like Albert's plan for Anglo-Prussian unity, it appeared to safeguard peace but required a puppet-master. That task fell to Victoria. It accounted for the voluminous correspondence she continued almost until her death, and those exhaustive portrait commissions through which, as with Ross's miniature of Albert so many years before, she asserted hegemony over her nearest and dearest: family likenesses by James Sant, Heinrich von Angeli, Carl Rudolph Sohn and Rudolph Swoboda, which proliferated during the final quarter of the century.

'What Queen in the world has been so rich in offspring and has such good cause to rejoice in her many children?' asked one observer in 1887.[5] In the first years of her marriage, Victoria had protested at the prospect of becoming 'mamma d'une nombreuse famille': those protests were short-lived. Quickly, unconsciously, she had learnt to exult in her vigorous brood. When her second daughter, Alice, died of diphtheria on the anniversary of Albert's death in 1878, aged only thirty-five, Victoria exclaimed painfully, 'I was so proud of my 9!'[6] Five years later, haemophiliac Leopold also died. He was thirty and had been married for two years. Yet the principal characteristic of Victoria and Albert's children was their robustness: all survived to adulthood and all but Louise presented Victoria with a clutch of grandchildren. By the end of her life, Victoria could boast more than seventy grandchildren and great-grandchildren. In time they would occupy the thrones of Britain, Germany, Spain, Russia, Norway, Greece, Romania, Yugoslavia, Sweden and Denmark. Through Coburg blood Victoria would be connected to the royal houses of Portugal, Belgium, Bulgaria, France, Austria and Italy, a commonwealth of royal kinship. Bishop Randall Davidson's statement in 1896, that Victoria wielded 'a personal and domestic influence over the thrones of Europe without precedent in the History of Christendom' could scarcely have surprised his canny sovereign: within that superb afflatus lay a simple truth.[7] Visiting Windsor Castle in 1899, the German Emperor William II, Victoria's eldest grandchild, stated with characteristic fanfaronade, 'From this Tower the World is ruled.'[8] He ought to have known. That very spring, Victoria warned Nicholas II of Russia, her grandson by marriage, of William's duplicity. She implored the Tsar for openness and confidentiality: 'It is so important that we should understand each other, and that such mischievous and unstraightforward proceedings should be put a stop to.'[9] Little wonder that another grandchild remembered 'Grandmama Queen' as 'the central power directing things'. The vision they shared was that of Kipling's 'The Widow at Windsor': 'For the Kings must come down and the Emperors frown/ When the Widow at Windsor says "Stop"!'

In May 1887, Victoria wrote to her third son, Arthur, describing a sketch recently completed by the Danish artist Laurits Regner Tuxen. It was a preliminary drawing for the large painting she had commissioned from Tuxen to commemorate the family gathering which would assemble that summer to celebrate her Golden Jubilee. Victoria's intention was for an image that combined decorative appeal with accurate likenesses. 'It is not to be stiff and according to *Etiquette*, but prettily grouped,' she explained.[10] The painting would also capture Victoria's twin roles of monarch and matriarch, a further instance of feminine stereotype invoked to qualify her 'masculine' sovereign power as a reigning queen.

The difficulties of Victoria's matriarchy swiftly emerged in Tuxen's efforts to attain his pretty grouping. The Danish-born Princess of Wales refused to stand next to the Crown Prince of Prussia; two decades after Prussia's part in the Schleswig-Holstein crisis, which had diminished her father's throne, Alix remained balefully anti-German. Arthur himself announced that he would rather be omitted from the painting than placed near his youngest sister Beatrice and her husband, Henry of Battenberg, whom she had been allowed to marry in 1885 after protracted struggles with her mother. Louise's husband, Lord Lorne, at first placed prominently on account of the picturesqueness of his Highland dress, was relegated to a less conspicuous position; instead visible Highland garb belongs to Affie's son, the higher-ranking Prince Alfred of Edinburgh. Despite Victoria's dismissal of 'Etiquette', the two most prominent men are Bertie and Fritz, respectively the Prince of Wales and German Crown Prince. As powerful as the family loyalties of Victoria's sons- and daughters-in-law were sibling rivalries among her own children. Happily such vituperation is absent from Tuxen's finished image, which Victoria described as 'beautiful, the Drawing room admirably painted and the likenesses very good . . . the grouping and colouring, all, charming'.[11] Yet no one was more conscious than she of the tensions that permeated her far-flung family. To her poet laureate Tennyson, she described her children as 'though all loving, [having] all their own interests and homes'. More than once she insisted that 'a large family is a great anxiety'; to Vicky she accounted it 'an immense difficulty & I must add – burthen to me!'[12] Today Tuxen's viewer is impressed above all by the size of Victoria's family, marshalled in superb plenitude in the Green Drawing Room at Windsor Castle. It was surely part of Victoria's intention. On three further occasions she commissioned similar group scenes from the artist. All assert unequivocally the grandeur and extent of Victoria's assembled dynasty.

Victoria's increasingly energetic interest in her family was symptomatic of that reinvigoration within her that took place during the second half of the 1870s. In part it arose from the passage of time, dispelling Albert's shade. Disraeli also played a part. His policy of awakening his Faery Queen worked *too* well. As contemporaries noted, having rubbed Aladdin's lamp so hard, he found it impossible again to banish the genie.

Crises in the Balkans, in which Disraeli supported the ailing Ottoman Empire as a bulwark against Russian expansion into southeast Europe, stimulated Victoria to a renewal of that overheated belligerence she had espoused during the Crimean War. In language, thought and action she disdained moderation. She was bellicose, adamant, emotive. As poet Alfred Austin described her after her death, 'She bore the trident, wore the helm.'[13] In 1877, she identified as her 'one object' 'the honour and dignity

of this country'.[14] Briefly she reprised her role of John
Bull in petticoats: the maintenance of 'honour and dignity'
demanded a vigorous show of pugnacity and strength.
'You say you hope we shall keep out of the [Russo-
Turkish] war and God knows I hope and pray and think
we shall – as to fighting,' she wrote to Vicky in June. 'But
I am sure you would not wish Great Britain to eat humble
pie to these horrible, deceitful, cruel Russians? I will not
be the sovereign to submit to that!'[15] Mostly she directed
her vigour towards inspiring Disraeli and his Cabinet. 'Be
bold!' she exhorted. For emphasis she threatened abdication
five times in ten months. Daily she bombarded the Prime
Minister with letters and telegrams. To the intense irritation
of Bertie, whom she continued to exclude from official
business, she resorted to employing in her machinations her
youngest son Leopold, a Conservative partisan who would
later represent her at Disraeli's funeral. His role as an extra
private secretary enabled Victoria to bypass Henry Ponsonby
with his Liberal sympathies and admonishments to a course
of greater caution.

For opinion in the country at large was divided. Gladstone
had re-emerged from retirement to lambast Turkish
atrocities against Bulgarian Christians: the ultimate victim
of his campaign, which included a bestselling pamphlet
The Bulgarian Horrors and the Question of the East, was
Disraeli. Victoria's line was nationalistic and patriotic: it
was also overtly party political. Priding herself on her
ability to judge the national mood and certain, as she
would always be, that her own wishes coincided with the
country's best interests, Victoria, like Disraeli,
miscalculated. The latter's resounding defeat at the polls
in 1880 was a catastrophe for his adoring and dependent
sovereign. 'What your loss to me as a Minister would be,
it is impossible to estimate,' she told him frankly.[16] Either

desperation or determination inspired her attempts to make Lord Hartington or Lord Granville prime minister; it was soon obvious that Gladstone must be invited to return. As in Melbourne's replacement by Peel, Victoria felt she could hardly bear it, 'a most disagreeable person – half crazy, and so excited'.[17] With unwitting irony she labelled him 'arrogant, tyrannical and obstinate'. His real crime was a perceived lack of regard for her own feelings (presumably in snatching victory against her will); later she would fulminate against 'the utter disregard of all my opinions which after 45 years of experience ought to be considered'.[18] In the short term, she concealed her chagrin behind more worthy concerns: 'The Queen cannot deny she . . . thinks it a great calamity for the country and the peace of Europe!'[19] To Ponsonby she suggested abdicating rather than working alongside her bête noire.

Happy for Victoria that she could not see into the future: the septuagenarian Gladstone still had three terms of office ahead of him. From 1880 to 1885, in 1886 and from 1892 to 1894, sovereign and premier consistently found causes of disagreement. Victoria's preoccupations remained foreign policy and, to a lesser extent, Ireland: both provided ample grounds for exasperation. Victoria cavilled at what she considered Liberal reluctance to maintain British prestige overseas (described by Victoria as a 'high tone'). Over Afghanistan, Egypt and the Sudan she berated the elected member. In January 1885, she held him person-ally responsible for the death of General Gordon, the maverick British commander charged with the defence of the Sudanese capital Khartoum, and took the unprecedented step of telegraphing her disapprobation to Gladstone and members of his Cabinet in a form guaranteed to leak the contents to the public. To Tennyson she wrote with her habitual bustle of 'the death of that noble Hero Gordon

(whose abandonment is an eternal blot on our crown
. . .)'.[20] As Laurence Housman's Victoria tells Bertie in
The Superlative Relative: 'In politics, and still more
in foreign policy, the less you rely on people's honour the
better.'[21] In private, she was polite, occasionally even
friendly towards her premier. She had invited him to
Arthur's wedding to Princess Louise Margaret of Prussia
in March 1879; invitations followed to Windsor Castle to
dine and sleep. Gladstone rightly attributed her behaviour
to her 'beautiful manners'[22] and did not confuse good
behaviour with kindliness or warmth of feeling. To his
wife he maintained, 'She will never be happy till She has
hounded me out of office' – an accurate estimation.[23] With
that goal beyond Victoria's reach, Gladstone discovered
that he had increasing occasion to find his thwarted royal
mistress 'somewhat unmannerly'.[24] On 30 January 1886,
Victoria invited Gladstone to form his third ministry only
after enquiries into her preferred option, a Whig–Tory
coalition under G. J. Goschen and Lord Salisbury, proved
fruitless. Six years later, as he prepared to take up office
for the fourth and last time, Victoria toyed with pre-empting
the Grand Old Man by sending for Lord Rosebery, who
she insisted be appointed Foreign Secretary.

In the event, Gladstone would plague her only briefly
in 1886. His government collapsed in June over proposals
for Irish Home Rule. Bluntly Victoria had made clear to
him the impossibility of her giving 'her Prime Minister
her full support . . . when the union of the Empire is in
danger of disintegration and serious disturbance'.[25] On
that occasion, Gladstone was replaced by Lord Salisbury,
'in whom she could confide, and whose opinion was always
given in so kind and wise a manner'.[26] Salisbury's admin-
istrations during Victoria's final years – from 1886 to
1892 and from 1895 to 1901 – were characterised by a

degree of harmony between monarch and premier every bit as sincere as her dislike for the 'deluded old fanatic' he replaced. Seeing them together, Lady Milner commented, 'I never saw two people get on better. Their polished manners and deference to and esteem for each other were a delightful sight and one not readily forgotten.'[27]

1886 was otherwise distinguished for Victoria by the public announcement of celebrations for her forthcoming Jubilee, scheduled to culminate in London on 21 June 1887, with a spectacular procession. From inception plans aroused controversy. Victoria's refusal to travel to Westminster Abbey in state or, as her son Arthur encouraged her, to make herself 'smart' in her velvet robes and crown, alongside government fears that overspending on the Jubilee would generate hostility, inspired plans dismissed by the *Standard* as 'utterly inadequate, mean, pinched and narrow'.[28] It was an unpromising beginning.

Victoria's first thoughts in connection with her Golden Jubilee were of loss. In her journal on 20 June 1886, she recorded: 'Have entered the fiftieth year of my reign and my Jubilee year. I was upset at the thought of those no longer with me, who would have been so pleased and happy, in particular my beloved husband, to whom I owe everything, who are gone to a happier world.'

Death had made its impress on the ageing Queen. Canon Baynes's 'Hymn for the Jubilee' asserted, 'It is not all of brightness/ That gathers round the Throne;/ The chalice of deep sorrow/ Full oft our Queen has known.'[29] From among her family and close circle not only Albert, but her mother, Melbourne, Uncle Leopold, Stockmar, her half-siblings Charles and Feodore, the Duke of Wellington ('so devoted, loyal, and faithful a subject, so staunch a supporter'),[30] Lehzen, Napoleon III, his only son Louis

Napoleon, Alice, Disraeli, John Brown and Leopold were all gone, a tidy rollcall of mourning obsequies. An inventory of recent deaths had dominated her journal entry for 31 December 1878, from the Kings of Saxony and Hanover to a child and a grandchild.[31] If Victoria had learnt lately to leaven her sadness with optimism, that sadness persisted. With grim punctilio she observed the anniversaries of those many deaths. Tokens of the departed – on canvas, in marble, bronze and silver gilt, in cairn and granite – clustered close about her like the trappings of an ancient pharaoh preparing to meet his gods in conclave. Her behaviour had changed during the last ten years: she remained recognisably the same. Only in her journal and in her letters is the gulf between the reality of a woman unable or unwilling ever fully to escape the shadows and the bland serenity of the mythologised Jubilee Queens of 1887 and 1897 so starkly revealed. Posterity has inherited a biscuit-tin vision of an elderly monarch who reigned, as Kipling has it, over ''alf o' Creation', with soft focus benignity: a gentle Britannia whose battles lay predominantly behind her. The truth was more complex. For while the Jubilee Queen of trinkets and penny eulogies basked in a glorious present, many of the real Victoria's thoughts – as Albert had identified so long ago – continued to be drawn ineluctably backwards.

With that backward glance came conflicting emotions. John Brown's death in the spring of 1883 inspired a second sortie into authorship. *More Leaves from the Journal of Our Life in the Highlands,* published in 1884, was dedicated to Victoria's 'devoted personal attendant and faithful friend'. Like *Leaves*, it was an elaborate homage to her yesterdays. Victoria's wreath on her servant's coffin had been inscribed, 'A tribute of loving, grateful and everlasting friendship from his truest, best and most faithful friend, Victoria R&I'.[32] The need for faithfulness in her relationships, and her insistence that they last for ever, represented a familiar impulse and one that would continue to cause her mingled joy and pain.

But the focus of the Golden Jubilee was the public rather than the private Victoria. For the first time commemorative stamps were issued. In booths lining the Strand, street vendors sold a patent automatic bustle which played 'God Save the Queen' when the wearer sat down. Carrying flambeaux and Japanese lanterns, Etonians processed through the Quadrangle of Windsor Castle, singing as they marched, 'Sing together, one and all/ Shout together, great and small/ Victoria! Victoria! Victoria! Our Queen!'[33] In London the sky glittered with a firework portrait of Victoria created by manufacturers James Pain & Sons, 180 feet high and 200 feet wide; technical glitches caused the right eye to flicker uncontrollably. Inscribed on the presentation box of the Golden Jubilee necklace of pearls and diamond trefoils purchased with donations from three million 'daughters of the Empire' and formally presented to Victoria, on 30 July 1888, by the Duchess of Buccleuch, was, 'To Victoria Queen & Empress A Token of Love & Loyalty from the Daughters of Her Empire in remembrance of Her Jubilee'.[34] Across the Empire, selected prison sentences were remitted in honour of the anniversary and Victoria's clemency: each was signed personally. Among cascades of telegrams came the acclamation, 'Empress of Hindoostan, Head of all Kings and Rulers, and King of all Kings, who is one in a Hundred, is Her Majesty Queen Victoria'.[35] All were tributes to a fifty-year reign. Perhaps only the necklace, which she herself had approved at the suggestion of the Women's Jubilee Offering Committee, touched Victoria personally: she was determined to avoid the short change of a brooch.

She did not admire ceremonial. She had no appetite for

the spectacular pageantry which, for an enthusiastic public, distinguished the last years of her reign. 'I don't want or like flattery,' she confided to her journal.[36] Mostly she meant it. As in 1872, when she had resisted Gladstone's plans for a public celebration of Bertie's recovery, she jibbed at the Jubilee proposals. As in 1872, her obstructiveness was overmastered. Lord Halifax protested that the public needed 'gilding for their money', Lord Rosebery that a bonnet rather than a diadem was inadequate apparel for the service of thanksgiving. Both men failed to recognise that the very homeliness of Victoria's dress, eschewing the swagger of her Continental cousins, could be deeply reassuring to those crowds of well-wishers who endorsed her domesticity but opposed the political engagement of more flaunting kings and princes. (Afterwards, Rosebery made good his lapse by presenting Victoria with a miniature of Elizabeth I and a 'flattering' letter. She admired the miniature while admitting, 'I fear I have no sympathy with my great predecessor.'[37]) The peers' criticisms made her nervous; they also served to remind her of who was Queen of England. In March, in high dudgeon, she wrote to Henry Ponsonby: 'The Queen hopes he will speak strongly to the Ministers, saying she will not be teased & bullied [about] the Jubilee & wh[ich] seems to be considered for the *people* & their *convenience* & amusement while the Queen is to do the public and newspapers bidding. She will do *nothing* if this goes on.'[38] It was the Jubilee equivalent of earlier abdication threats and similarly empty. It suggested too the grieving Victoria of the 1860s, for whom duty was a matter of inclination.

On 21 June, after a day of entertaining 'all the Royalties' at Buckingham Palace – sovereigns and their suites from Savoy to Siam – she drove in an open landau with an escort of Indian cavalry to Westminster Abbey. Surrounded by a mob of royal relations, enormous crowds and what she described as 'such an extraordinary outburst of enthusiasm as I had hardly ever seen in London before',[39] Victoria nevertheless found time for bereftness: 'I sat alone (oh! without my beloved husband, for whom this would have been such a proud day) . . .' The previous morning, in a journal entry which recalls that of the first day of her reign, she told herself, 'The day has come, and I am alone, though surrounded by many dear children.'[40] That reiterated 'alone' was more than empty rhetoric, a linguistic tic acquired through long habit, transformed by the events of 1861 from exultation to despair. It expressed enduring truths about Victoria's view of queenship and something of her detachment from the glittering but unwelcome roundelay of which she found herself the centre. Four years would pass before she took delivery of the painting she had commissioned from John Charlton of *The Golden Jubilee, 21 June 1887: The Royal Procession Passing Trafalgar Square*, with its careful delineation of happy, pilchard-tin crowds and ceremonial uniforms. On receipt it hung briefly at Windsor Castle. Afterwards it was removed to Buckingham Palace, the home Victoria avoided. Its fate was markedly different from that of Tuxen's painting, in which a domestic Victoria, plumply affectionate, is surrounded by her family: 'mother of many nations', 'Grandmama of Europe'. It was exactly as the public wished it. In its post-Jubilee commentary, *The Spectator* noted that the popular attitude to Victoria demonstrated 'a change indescribable, but unmistakable; an increase of kindliness and affection, but a decrease of awe. It was a friend of all who was welcomed, rather than a great Sovereign.'[41]

The death of a dog was the subject of a letter from Victoria to her granddaughter, the former Princess Victoria of

Hesse, in the autumn of 1887. In the aftermath of the Jubilee came this unlooked-for blow. 'It is indeed a grievous loss to me of a *real* friend whom I miss terribly,' Victoria wrote.[42] Noble was a favourite among her many dogs, described in the photograph album devoted to the royal kennels as 'a collie of the Cheviot breed'.[43] He had been given to Victoria at Balmoral on 24 May 1872, as spring turned to summer following the seismic shift attendant on Bertie's recovery. Fifteen years later, his death on 18 September inspired gloomy reflections on the part of a still-lonely woman who, half a century ago, at a moment of similar rejoicing, had returned from her coronation in Westminster Abbey, cast aside her robes and hurried upstairs to bathe her beloved spaniel Dash.

11

'All that magnificence'

Like many publicly modest people, Victoria was capable of conceit in private. On 23 September 1896, she noted in her journal: 'Today is the day on which I have reigned longer, by a day, than any English sovereign.'[1] She dismissed ideas of public commemoration. Exertions of that variety must wait until the Jubilee of the following summer, for she recognised, even if she could not embrace it, that 'English people . . . like all that magnificence, just as they like descriptions of jewels or scenes in the "Arabian Nights",' and it could not be shirked indefinitely.[2]

Yet it was not her preferred expression of sovereignty. For that she had three more years to wait, until the outbreak of the Boer War in October 1899. At first, that distant and unlovely conflict energised the octogenarian Queen into her customary martial bravado. From her wheelchair she inspected troops, a lump in her throat as she waved off the Gordon Highlanders, and that Christmas authorised for those same brave fighting men the distribution in her name of 100,000 tins of chocolate. In time she visited the inevitable wounded. Famously she asserted to future prime minister, A. J. Balfour, 'We are

not interested in the possibilities of defeat; they do not
exist,' though in private the war news caused her acute
anxiety, the casualty lists reducing her to tears. Plagued
by rheumatism and poor digestion, her eyesight failing
rapidly, her mobility strenuously impaired, she summoned
that spirit which had stirred her during the Crimean War,
through the Balkan Crises of the 1870s and in trenchant
dealings with any number of her ministers and children
ever since. Her private secretary claimed that she was all
'in favour of teaching Kruger [the Boer president] a sharp
lesson';[3] high casualties, unexpected reversals and the
creeping passage of time awakened in her a sense of war's
futility. On the Continent, caricaturists hostile to Britain
pounced on what they regarded as Victoria's bellicose and
acquisitive intent. With partial accuracy they attributed
to her aspects of the braggadocio and greed of her swollen
empire, proof of the extent to which she had become a
symbol, a figurehead Queen of England. In 1882, the *Daily
Telegraph* had described Victoria as ruler 'of the greatest
and mightiest empire ever submitted to a woman's sway'.[4]
In 1899, that 'woman's sway' combined compassion with
conviction and the yearning for victory of a soldier's
daughter, as well as the natural feelings of wife, mother
and grandmother. (Helena's soldier son Prince Christian
Victor of Schleswig-Holstein, called Christle, died of
enteric fever at Pretoria in October 1900. The news
reduced Victoria to sleeplessness and an infantile diet of
arrowroot and milk.[5]) She celebrated victories at Kimberley
and Ladysmith and eventually, in May 1900, the relief of
Mafeking, but she died before the cessation of hostilities
and confirmation of British victory in the costly Treaty
of Vereeniging in May 1902. Among her final official
duties had been an audience with Lord Roberts, former
British commander and victor of Paardeberg, Poplar

Grove, Diamond Hill and Bergendal. She conferred upon him the Order of the Garter.

Before the Boers, Victoria found herself embroiled in fighting of a different order. It was the final instance of that maladroit approach to her own domestic affairs which had previously threatened her early married life, when she pitted Lehzen against Albert, and the years of her seclusion, when she failed to check the boorishness of John Brown and so imposed upon her household and her intimates a tyranny more exacting than her own obdurate caprice.

The offender on this occasion was a twenty-four-year-old *khidmutgar*, or male waiter, called Abdul Karim. He was one of two Indian attendants sent to Victoria in May 1887 by Sir John Tyler, governor of India's Northwest Provinces. Victoria described him as 'tall, and with a fine serious countenance';[6] afterwards she added that he was 'a *perfect* gentleman' and 'in every way such a high-minded and excellent young man'.[7] Events would show that she was mistaken. Neither her family nor her household shared her estimation of the blandly supercilious outsider, who quickly acquired the favoured status of 'a sort of pet, like a dog or cat which the Queen will not willingly give up'.[8] Victoria did indeed treat Karim as a pet. She commissioned his portrait on at least four occasions, including, in the summer of his arrival, from Tuxen, then engaged in the eight-month process of painting *The Family of Queen Victoria in 1887*. She herself made a painstaking copy in watercolours of a portrait executed in 1888 by Rudolph Swoboda, one of her last and best, and hung his photograph with that of John Brown in her dressing room. She presented Karim with houses at Frogmore and Osborne and the purpose-built Karim Cottage at

Balmoral. Persuaded by his story that his father was a surgeon-general in the Indian Army and he himself a well-paid clerk, Victoria was inveigled into releasing him from serving duties. Instead she appointed him her *munshi*, or Indian secretary. In return he taught her Hindustani. Her Hindustani diaries survive in the Royal Archives.

Inevitably Karim was none of the things he had claimed for himself. Nor did his character correspond with Victoria's verdict of gentlemanliness, high-mindedness or excellence. He was dishonest, overbearing, silly and self-important. Sexually promiscuous, he contracted gonorrhoea. He stole a brooch belonging to Victoria and was suspected of leaking sensitive information about British policy in India to anti-British organisations. Protests were made: Victoria refused to listen.

Throughout her life, strength of opposition served merely to stiffen her resolve. So it proved again in the case of Abdul Karim. Victoria's love affair with India was of long duration. Her engagement with the subcontinent was imaginative, romantic, possessive, fanciful, but kindly. As she wrote to one of her daughters-in-law, 'I have *such* a great longing sometime to go to India.'[9] It was not to be. Instead fragments of India travelled to her: aside from her Indian attendants, her ivory throne; historic jewels of cursed and bloody history; illuminated manuscripts; hostages to fortune like Dalip Singh, the dispossessed Maharaja of the Punjab, who settled in Gloucestershire on a government pension, and Princess Gouramma of Coorg, flirtatious and consumptive, an unlikely goddaughter for Victoria. In 1890–91 she added the Durbar Room to Osborne House, inspired by Arthur's cod-Indian billiard room at Bagshot Park and the need for a state entertaining space. An icing sugar confection of fretted and snowy plasterwork undertaken under the supervision of Kipling's father, its scale was suitably imperial. Its design made concessions to authenticity: its carpet was woven in the women's prison at Agra, its curtains of coarse cloth hand-blocked with an Indian-inspired paisley motif. At Osborne and elsewhere, including the spring holidays to Italy and the South of France which were a feature of her last years, Victoria insisted that her Indian attendants, like her Highlanders, wore native costume at all times. Balmoral winters necessitated 'native' fashions made from tweed.

At one level, Karim was another exotic trophy for this ageing empress and commended to her by his dark good looks; he also delighted her with knowledge and understanding of the country she was unable to visit in person. Unusually for her time, Victoria was without racial prejudice. Emphatically she expressed 'her very strong feeling (and she had few stronger) that the natives and coloured races should be treated with every kindness and affection, as brothers, not – as, alas! Englishmen too often do – as totally different to ourselves . . .'[10] In 1898, she complained that Indians were under-represented in the Birthday Honours. As she soon discovered, neither household nor relatives shared her enlightenment. At court, complaints about Karim proliferated: he was 'bland, smiling, furtive and scheming'.[11] The gentlemen of the household refused to associate with him on terms of equality, the women recoiled from his serpentine presence. 'I am for ever meeting him in passages or the garden or face to face on the stairs,' recorded maid of honour Marie Mallet in 1899, 'and each time I shudder more.'[12] It was trivial and unedifying, snobbish and distasteful. Victoria was predictably unamused. In her disgruntlement she grew formidable, once sweeping every object from her desk in her fury at another row about the *munshi*.

The more frequent the complaints against Karim, the stronger grew Victoria's conviction that her household's objections arose from racist motives. She considered too that her hand was being forced – always a counterproductive approach. The result was an impasse. Karim himself provided a resolution of sorts. A photograph appeared in *The Daily Graphic* in October 1897: Victoria sits at her desk signing documents, while Karim looks on, impassive and majestic. It was a reversal of the true order of their relationship, an affront consolidated by the caption: 'The Queen's Life in the Highlands, Her Majesty receiving a lesson in Hindustani from the Munshi Hafiz Abdul Karim C.I.E.'.[13] To her doctor Victoria admitted that she had been made to look foolish. Still Karim remained a fixture. Increasingly he fought his battles not with those equerries who spurned him but with Victoria herself, unable to restrain his overbearingness. A bemused Lord Salisbury concluded that Victoria enjoyed the 'emotional excitement' of their sparring.

This was not, however, a decade of anger and embitterment; as Lytton Strachey described them, these were the years of apotheosis.[14] Victoria had fought hard to prevent her youngest daughter Beatrice from marrying. That marriage, to Prince Henry of Battenberg, called 'Liko', solemnised on the Isle of Wight in 1885, breathed new life into Victoria's moribund court. Liko was handsome and patient. He treated his mother-in-law with skittish deference. She in turn described him as 'like a bright sunbeam in My Home'.[15] The couple lived continually at Victoria's side, in apartments created specially for them in Osborne's Durbar wing. Victoria took up dancing again. Again she sang duets, breaking off to remind her audience that her singing masters had included Mendelssohn. Again she watched plays. It was Bertie who reintroduced his mother to the theatre: command performances again became a feature of court life. Again there were tableaux vivants, elaborately costumed, prepared for over several weeks, again Victoria's children taking the principal parts as they had in similar tableaux while Albert was alive, now joined by grandchildren too: Beatrice as a matronly Queen of Sheba; Bertie's eldest son Eddy as Charles Edward the Young Pretender; the future Tsarina of Russia, Princess Alix of Hesse, in the guise of novice nun. In November 1891, following a performance of *Cavalleria Rusticana* in the Waterloo Gallery at Windsor Castle, Victoria noted, 'I had not heard an Italian opera for thirty-one years . . . I loved the music.'[16] It was a return to happiness – amid the anniversaries of deaths an acknowledgement of many blessings. To Marie Mallet, Victoria confessed that she who had once prayed to die now clung to life.

And yet steadily the death toll mounted. On 14 January 1892, days after his twenty-eighth birthday and within weeks of his proposed wedding to Princess May of Teck, Bertie's son Albert Victor, Duke of Clarence and Avondale, known as Eddy, died of pneumonia: he ought to have succeeded his grandmother and father as king. So enfeebled was Jane, Lady Ely, by a widowhood in Victoria's service that she was unable to manage her knife and fork by the time of her death in June 1890: to her employer's surprise, her food was cut up for her.[17] Overwork similarly claimed Victoria's private secretary Sir Henry Ponsonby, who died in November 1895 following a severe stroke, after quarter of a century's devoted service. Smarting under his ornamental existence as courtly swain, Liko escaped to Africa and the Ashanti War against King Prempeh. He swiftly contracted malaria and died on 20 January 1896. Most trying of all had been the death from cancer of the larynx of Vicky's husband Fritz, after a reign of only ninety-nine days in 1888. The demise of the 'Barbarossa of German liberalism', a personal blow to Victoria, also spelled the death knell to Albert's tattered dreams of Anglo-German unity. Fritz's successor, William II, treated his grandmother with outward respect while espousing on Germany's behalf policies of inconsistency and vainglory, which nurtured dangerous tensions between the two empires. The outcome of those tensions in 1914 was shielded from Victoria.

Instead one last huzzah awaited her: her Diamond Jubilee, the first in British history. Even its name was a new coinage by private secretary Arthur Bigge, in preference to 'Jubilissimee', 'Jubilificence' and 'The Queen's Commemoration'. A decade previously, at a Golden Jubilee party for schoolchildren in Hyde Park, Victoria had received a bouquet. Attached was an embroidered message, 'God bless our Queen, not Queen alone, but Mother, Queen and friend'.[18] At the suggestion of Colonial Secretary Joseph Chamberlain, once mistrusted by Victoria as 'Gladstone's evil genius', the Diamond Jubilee would celebrate Victoria as imperial 'mother', a matriarchy greater and grander than her role as Grandmama of Europe. 'There has never been in English territory any representation of the Empire as a whole,' Chamberlain told Lord Salisbury, 'and the Colonies especially have, hitherto, taken little part in any ceremony of the kind.'[19] Victoria released an official Jubilee photograph in which cascades of Honiton lace lightened her widow's weeds and extensive diamonds imbued with an appropriately sombre magnificence this sovereign of 200 million world-wide subjects;[20] the photograph itself had been taken four years earlier. Before she left Buckingham Palace for the short celebration of thanksgiving outside St Paul's Cathedral – Victoria was too lame to mount the cathedral steps and remained in her carriage – she telegraphed a message across her far-flung Empire: 'From my heart I thank my beloved people, May God bless them!' In their thousands, her beloved people lined the streets to cheer her. 'No one ever, I believe, has met with such an ovation as was given to me, passing through those six miles of streets.'[21] Colonial troops were among soldiers lining the way; they also packed the cathedral precincts. 'Until we saw it passing through the streets of our city we never quite realised what the Empire meant,' exulted the *Daily Mail*.[22] According to *The Spectator*, 'The note of the entire festivity was imperialism.'[23]

Victoria died on 22 January 1901 at Osborne House on the Isle of Wight. The century died with her; so too that palace by the sea, built by Victoria and Albert and never again a royal home. Her children and her grandchildren were at her bedside, her final hours every bit as public as those of her husband or indeed as any of the significant moments of her long and necessarily prominent life. She died, as she had lived and reigned, outwardly assertive, honest in her self-appraisal, 'in peace with all, fully aware of my many faults',[24] but reluctant, when it came to it, finally to relinquish control.

'The afternoon of the 21st was a most disturbing time,' Lord Lorne wrote to Tennyson's son, Hallam. 'The breathing seemed so often clogged, and the intimation was several times made by the Doctor that the death must come, and still it could not come, the strong heart still resisting the attack. My wife was on her knees for nearly 4 hours holding her mother's hand.'[25] At the end, Victoria's final thoughts were of her husband, her last words: 'Oh, Albert . . .'

In death she lies alongside Albert in the mausoleum she herself constructed. While the Albert of Marochetti's tomb effigy gazes heavenward, his Victoria turns her face towards him.

NOTES

INTRODUCTION

1 David Thomson, *England in the Nineteenth Century* (Penguin reprint, London, 1986), p. 169.
2 Ibid., p. 169.
3 Ibid., p. 170.
4 Giles St Aubyn, *Queen Victoria: A Portrait* (Sinclair Stevenson, London, 1991), p. 169.
5 Walter Bagehot (ed. Miles Taylor), *The English Constitution* (Oxford World Classics reprint, Oxford, 2009), p. 34.

CHAPTER ONE

1 Walter L. Arnstein, *Queen Victoria* (Palgrave Macmillan, Basingstoke, 2003), p. 131.
2 *Manchester Guardian*, 24 June 1837.
3 Cecil Woodham-Smith, *Victoria 1819–1861* (Hamish Hamilton, London, 1972), p. 47.
4 Mrs Oliphant, *Queen Victoria: A Personal Sketch* (Cassell and Company, London, 1901), p. 1.
5 Kate Williams, *Becoming Queen* (Hutchinson, London, 2008), p. 157.

6 Lynne Vallone, *Becoming Victoria* (Yale University Press, 2001), p. 1.

7 Dormer Creston, *The Youthful Queen Victoria* (Macmillan & Co., London, 1952), p. 23.

8 Ibid., p. 85.

9 David Duff, *Edward of Kent* (Frederick Muller reprint, London, 1973), p. 164.

10 Venetia Murray, *High Society in the Regency Period* (Penguin, London, 1999), p. 18.

11 Woodham-Smith, op. cit., p. 28.

12 Elizabeth Longford, *Victoria RI* (Weidenfeld & Nicolson, London, 1964), p. 20.

13 Flora Fraser, *Princesses: The Six Daughters of George III* (John Murray, London, 2004), p. 321.

14 Margaret Homans, and Adrienne Munich, eds., *Remaking Queen Victoria* (Cambridge University Press, Cambridge, 1997), p. 60.

15 RA Geo 45503–4, quoted Vallone, op. cit., p. 3.

16 John Raymond, ed., *Queen Victoria's Early Letters* (Batsford, London, 1963).

17 RA M4–26, Duchess of Kent to Earl Grey, 28 January 1831.

18 Roger Fulford, ed., *Dearest Child: Letters from Queen Victoria and the Princess Royal, 1858–1861* (Evans Brothers, London, 1964), p. 125.

19 Theo Aronson, *Grandmama of Europe* (John Murray paperback, London, 1984), p. 7.

20 Vallone, op. cit., p. 3.

21 Ibid., p. 19.

22 Duff, op. cit., p. 287.

CHAPTER TWO

1 W. H. Hudson, *Birds in London* (Longmans, Green and Co., London, 1898), see pp. 77–85.

2 Creston, op. cit., p. 65.

3 Vallone, op. cit., p. 200.

4 Arnstein, op. cit., p. 24.

5 Elizabeth Barrett, 'Victoria's Tears'.

6 St Aubyn, op. cit., p. 121.

7 Katherine Hudson, *A Royal Conflict: Sir John Conroy and the Young Victoria* (Hodder & Stoughton, London, 1994), p. 16.

8 See Fraser, op. cit., p. 360.

9 Creston, op. cit., p. 83.

10 Malcolm Johnson, *Bustling Intermeddler? The Life and Work of Charles James Blomfield* (Gracewing paperback, Leominster, 2001), p. 41.

11 Stanley Weintraub, *Victoria: Biography of a Queen* (Unwin, London, 1987), p. 56.

12 Vallone, op. cit., p. 45.

13 Edgar Feuchtwanger, *Albert and Victoria: The Rise and Fall of the House of Saxe-Coburg-Gotha* (Hambledon Continuum, London, 2006), p. 9.

14 Homans, op. cit., p. 61.

15 RA VIC M5/19, quoted Vallone, op. cit., p. 72.

16 RA VIC/MAIN/Z/111, p. 7.

17 Theodore Martin, *Queen Victoria As I Knew Her* (William Blackwood and Sons, Edinburgh and London, 1908), p. 64.

18 Vallone, op. cit., p. 20.

19 Weintraub, op. cit., p. 63.

20 Arnstein, op. cit., p. 21.

21 Longford, op. cit., p. 48.

22 Dorothy Marshall, *The Life and Times of Queen Victoria* (Weidenfeld & Nicolson, London, 1972), p. 30.

23 RA VIC 61/22.

24 RA VIC/MAIN/Y/203/81.

25 Laurence Housman, *Happy and Glorious: A Dramatic Biography* (The Reprint Society, London, 1943), p. 9.

26 Richard Williams, *The Contentious Crown: Public Discussion of the British Monarchy in the Reign of Queen Victoria* (Ashgate, Aldershot, 1997), p. 193.

27 Feuchtwanger, op. cit., p. 11.

28 Stanley Weintraub, *Albert Uncrowned King* (John Murray paperback, London, 1998), p. 57.

CHAPTER THREE

1 Oliphant, op. cit., p. 27.

2 Charles Greville, quoted Oliphant, op. cit., p. 29; Creston, op. cit., p. 263.

3 Martin, op. cit., p. 65.

4 Raymond, op. cit., p. 19.

5 Lytton Strachey, *Queen Victoria* (Chatto & Windus reprint, London, 1928), p. 50.

6 Raymond, op. cit., p. 23.

7 Fraser, op. cit., p. 366.

8 K. D. Reynolds, and H. C. G. Matthew, *Queen Victoria* (Oxford University Press, Oxford, 2007), p. 14.

9 See Kate Williams, op. cit., p. 38.

10 Reynolds, op. cit., p. 16.

11 John Plunkett, *Queen Victoria, First Media Monarch* (Oxford University Press, Oxford, 2003), p. 97.

12 Ibid., p. 132.

13 Kate Williams, op. cit., p. 267.

14 *Manchester Guardian*, 24 June 1837.

15 Quoted Rev. Charles Bullock, *The Queen's Resolve: A Jubilee Memorial* (Home Words Publishing, London, 1887), p. 39.

16 St Aubyn, op. cit., p. 87.

17 Longford, op. cit., p. 101.

18 Vallone, op. cit., p. 100.

19 Christopher Hibbert, *Queen Victoria: A Personal History* (HarperCollins, London, 2000), p. 50.

20 Feuchtwanger, op. cit., p. 18.

21 Longford, op. cit., p. 112.

22 Alfred Tennyson, 'Dedication to the Queen'.

23 Martin, op. cit., pp. 60–61

CHAPTER FOUR

1 Oliver Millar, *The Victorian Paintings in the Collection of Her Majesty the Queen* (Cambridge University Press, Cambridge, 1992), p. 67.

2 Matthew Dennison, *The Last Princess: The Devoted Life of Queen Victoria's Youngest Daughter* (Weidenfeld & Nicolson, London, 2007), p. 23.

3 St Aubyn, op. cit., p. 125.

4 Marina Warner, *Queen Victoria's Sketchbook* (Macmillan, London, 1979), p. 59.

5 RA VIC/MAIN/Y/88/15.

6 Weintraub, op. cit. (*Albert Uncrowned King*), p. 78.

7 Ibid., p. 86.

8 Housman, op. cit., p. 90.

9 Quoted Weintraub, op. cit. (*Victoria*), p. 133.

10 Warner, op. cit., p. 87.

11 Jeanne Cannizzo, *Our Highland Home: Victoria and Albert in Scotland* (National Galleries of Scotland, Edinburgh, 2005), p. 7.

12 Longford, op. cit., p. 136.

13 Jonathan Marsden, ed., *Victoria and Albert: Art and Love* (Royal Collections Publications, London, 2010), p. 55.

14 Ibid.

15 George Rowell, *Queen Victoria Goes to the Theatre* (Paul Elek, London, 1978), p. 20.

16 Weintraub, op. cit. (*Albert Uncrowned King*), p. 126.

17 Longford, op. cit., p. 130.

18 Kate Williams, op. cit., p. 235.

CHAPTER FIVE

1 Andrew Sinclair, *The Other Victoria: The Princess Royal and the Great Game of Europe* (Weidenfeld & Nicolson, London, 1981).

2 Marsden, op. cit., p. 26.

3 Warner, op. cit., p. 103.

4 Raymond, op. cit., p. 188.

5 Martin, op. cit., p. 36.

6 John Ruskin, *Of Queens' Gardens.*

7 Housman, op. cit., p. 103.

8 Feuchtwanger, op. cit., p. 67.

9 Ibid., p. 45.

10 Warner, op. cit., p. 134.

11 Vallone, op. cit., p. 152.

12 Richard Williams, op. cit., p. 195.

13 Marsden, op. cit., p. 26.

14 Millar, op. cit., p. 83.

15 Marsden, op. cit., p. 397.

16 Queen Victoria to the Crown Princess of Prussia, 28 July 1875, quoted Millar, op. cit., p. 5.

17 Homans, op. cit., p. 83.

18 Plunkett, op. cit., pp. 100–01.

19 Richard Williams, op. cit., p. 25.

20 Weintraub, op. cit. (*Albert Uncrowned King*), p. 181.

21 Queen Victoria's Journal, 9 October 1857.

22 RA VIC/MAIN/M/12/55.

23 Dennison, op. cit., pp. 15–16.

24 Jane Ridley, *Bertie: A Life of Edward VII* (Chatto & Windus, London, 2012), p. 13.

25 Kate Hubbard, *Serving Victoria: Life in the Royal Household* (Chatto & Windus, London, 2012), p. 160.

26 Kate Williams, op. cit., p. 331.

27 Roger Fulford, ed., *Dearest Mama: Letters Between Queen Victoria and the Crown Princess of Prussia 1861–64* (Evans Brothers, London, 1968), p. 23.

28 Plunkett, op. cit., p. 46.

29 St Aubyn, op. cit., p. 217.

30 Michael De-la-Noy, *Queen Victoria at Home* (Constable & Robinson, London, 2003), p. 175.

31 Longford, op. cit., p. 226.

32 Raymond, op. cit., p. 204.

33 Ibid., p. 205.

34 Ibid., p. 216.

35 Marshall, op. cit., p. 114.

36 Arnstein, op. cit., p. 99.

37 Benita Stoney, and Heinrich C. Weltzein, *My Mistress the Queen: The Letters of Frieda Arnold, Dresser to Queen Victoria, 1854–59*, trans. Sheila de Bellaigue (Weidenfeld & Nicolson, London, 1994), p. 102.

38 Homans, op. cit., p. 72.

39 Longford, op. cit., p. 261.

CHAPTER SIX

1 Weintraub, op. cit. (*Albert Uncrowned King*), p. 191.

2 Sinclair, op. cit., p. 33.

3 Fulford, ed., op. cit. (*Dearest Child*), p. 27.

4 Ibid., p. 95.

5 Ibid., p. 31.

6 Ibid., p. 124.

7 St Aubyn, op. cit., p. 270.

8 Fulford, ed., op. cit. (*Dearest Child*), p. 96 (fn).

9 Millar, op. cit., pp. 297–98.

10 Dean of Windsor, and Hector Bolitho, eds., *Letters of Lady Augusta Stanley* (George Howe, London, 1927), p. 169.

11 Longford, op. cit., p. 290.

12 Fulford, ed., op. cit. (*Dearest Child*), p. 319.

13 Ibid., p. 320.

14 Ibid., p. 324.

15 Aronson, op. cit., p. 22.

16 Warner, op. cit., p. 158.

17 Fulford, ed., op. cit. (*Dearest Child*), pp. 369–70.

18 Millar, op. cit., p. 315.

19 Weintraub, op. cit. (*Victoria*), p. 305.

20 Helmut Gernsheim, and Alison Gernsheim, *Queen Victoria* (Longmans, Green and Co., London, 1959), p. 63.

21 Marsden, op. cit., p. 70.

22 Martyn Downer, *The Queen's Knight* (Bantam Press, London, 2007), p. 66.

23 Ridley, op. cit., p. 21.

24 Oliphant, op. cit., p. 108.

25 Longford, op. cit., p. 296.

26 Bullock, op. cit., p. 104.

27 Fulford, ed., op. cit. (*Dearest Child*), p. 374.

CHAPTER SEVEN

1 Helen Rappaport, *Magnificent Obsession: Victoria, Albert and the Death that Changed the Monarchy* (Hutchinson, London, 2011), p. 99.

2 Hibbert, op. cit., p. 160.

3 Ibid., p. 161.

4 Gernsheim, op. cit., p. 140.

5 Hibbert, op. cit., p. 45.

6 Longford, op. cit., p. 307.

7 Daphne Bennett, *King without a Crown* (Heinemann, London, 1977), p. 375.

8 Arnstein, op. cit., p. 109.

9 Hibbert, op. cit., p. 192.

10 Rappaport, op. cit., p. 169.

11 Gernsheim, op. cit., p. 62.

12 Rappaport, op. cit., p. 169.

13 Ibid., p. 173.

14 Marsden, op. cit., p. 332.

15 Marshall, op. cit., p. 164.

16 Raymond, op. cit., p. 292.

17 Plunkett, op. cit., p. 180.

18 Longford, op. cit., p. 308.

19 Hibbert, op. cit., p. 163.

20 Ibid., p. 161.

21 Ibid., p. 178.

22 Dean of Windsor, and Bolitho, eds., op. cit., pp. 258–59.

23 Fulford, ed., op. cit. (*Dearest Mama*), p. 24.

24 Hibbert, op. cit., p. 171.

25 Gail Turley Houston, *Royalties: The Queen and Victorian Writers* (University Press of Virginia, Charlottesville and London, 1999), p. 148.

26 Fulford, ed., *Your Dear Letter: Private Correspondence of Queen Victoria and the Crown Princess of Prussia, 1856–71* (Evans Brothers, London, 1971), p. 209.

27 Vallone, op. cit., p. 14.

28 St Aubyn, op. cit., p. 412.

29 Hibbert, op. cit., p. 193.

30 Fulford, ed., op. cit. (*Dearest Mama*), p. 62.

31 Hope Dyson, and Charles Tennyson, eds., *Dear and Honoured Lady: The Correspondence Between Queen Victoria and Alfred Tennyson* (Macmillan, London, 1969), p. 105.

32 Hibbert, op. cit., p. 186.

33 George Earle Buckle, ed., *The Letters of Queen Victoria 1879–85*, second series (John Murray, London, 1928), p. 298.

34 Vallone, op. cit., p. xvi.

CHAPTER EIGHT

1 Millar, op. cit., p. 13.
2 Tom Cullen, *The Empress Brown: The Story of a Royal Friendship* (The Bodley Head, London, 1969), p. 50.
3 John van der Kiste, *Sons, Servants and Statesmen: The Men in Queen Victoria's Life* (Sutton, Stroud, 2006), p. 116.
4 Longford, op. cit., p. 325.
5 St Aubyn, op. cit., p. 356.
6 Fulford, ed., op. cit. (*Your Dear Letter*), p. 18.
7 Dennison, op. cit., p. 46.
8 Millar, op. cit., p. 147.
9 Ibid., p. 147.
10 Dennison, op. cit., p. 51.
11 Cullen, op. cit., p. 102.
12 Ibid., p. 103.
13 Richard Williams, op. cit., p. 34.
14 Weintraub, op. cit. (*Victoria*), p. 374.
15 St Aubyn, op. cit., p. 330.
16 Raymond Lamont-Brown, *John Brown, Queen Victoria's Highland Servant* (Sutton, Stroud, 2000), p. 152.
17 Fulford, ed., op. cit. (*Your Dear Letter*), p. 23.
18 Ibid., p. 22.
19 Ibid., p. 203.
20 Weintraub, op. cit. (*Victoria*), p. 381.
21 Longford, op. cit., p. 326.

CHAPTER NINE

1 Earl of Bessborough, *Lady Charlotte Schreiber, Extracts from Her Journal 1853–1891* (John Murray, London, 1952), p. 74.
2 Richard Williams, op. cit., p. 216.
3 Longford, op. cit., p. 565.

4 Lytton Strachey, *Queen Victoria* (Chatto & Windus reprint, London, 1928), p. 221.

5 St Aubyn, op. cit., p. 377.

6 Helen Rappaport, *Queen Victoria: A Biographical Companion* (ABC Clio, 2003), p. 56.

7 St Aubyn, op. cit., p. 363.

8 Ridley, op. cit., p. 120.

9 Hibbert, op. cit., p. 209.

10 Arthur Ponsonby, *Henry Ponsonby, Queen Victoria's Private Secretary: His Life from His Letters* (Macmillan & Co., London, 1943), p. 184.

11 Millar, op. cit., p. 5.

12 Ponsonby, op. cit., p. 73.

13 Longford, op. cit., p. 421.

14 Dennison, op. cit., p. 75.

15 Longford, op. cit., p. 383.

16 Weintraub, op. cit. (*Victoria*), p. 367.

17 Paul Thomas Murphy, *Shooting Victoria: Madness, Mayhem and the Modernisation of the Monarchy* (Head of Zeus, London, 2012), p. 355.

18 Ibid., p. 356.

19 Richard Hough, *Edward & Alexandra: Their Private and Public Lives* (Hodder & Stoughton, London, 1993), p. 139.

20 Dennison, op. cit., p. 77.

21 Hibbert, op. cit., p. 213.

22 Ibid., p. 213.

23 Ridley, op. cit., p. 153.

24 Hough, op. cit., p. 146.

25 Ibid., p. 149.

26 Hibbert, op. cit., p. 216.

27 Longford, op. cit., p. 404.

28 Marsden, op. cit., p. 330.

29 Ponsonby, op. cit., p. 141.

30 Sophie Gilmartin, *Ancestry and Narrative in Nineteenth-Century British Literature: Blood Relations from Edgeworth to Hardy* (CUP paperback, Cambridge, 2005), p. 118.

31 Richard Williams, op. cit., p. 173.

32 Hibbert, op. cit., p. 242.

33 Longford, op. cit., p. 427.

34 Feuchtwanger, op. cit., p. 179.

35 Millar, op. cit., pp. 209–14.

CHAPTER TEN

1 Buckle, op. cit., vol. 3, p. 18.

2 Ibid.

3 Fulford, ed., op. cit. (*Your Dear Letter*), pp. 200–01.

4 Dennison, op. cit., p. 23; Bullock, op. cit., p. 102.

5 Aronson, op. cit., p. 6.

6 Longford, op. cit., p. 425.

7 St Aubyn, op. cit., 603.

8 Ibid., p. 608.

9 Hibbert, op. cit., p. 338.

10 Millar, op. cit., p. 270.

11 Queen Victoria's Journal, 1 December 1887, Millar, op. cit., p. 271.

12 Dyson and Tennyson, eds., op. cit., p. 104; Longford, op. cit., p. 421.

13 Arnstein, op. cit., p. 201.

14 Fulford, ed., *Darling Child: Private Correspondence of Queen Victoria and the Crown Princess of Prussia, 1871–78* (Evans Brothers, London, 1976), p. 251.

15 Hibbert, op. cit., p. 245.

16 Buckle, op. cit., vol. 3, p. 75.

17 Weintraub, op. cit. (*Victoria*), p. 445.

18 Buckle, op. cit., vol. 3, p. 298.

19 Ibid., p. 73.

20 Dyson and Tennyson, eds., op. cit., p. 118.

21 Housman, op. cit., p. 415.

22 St Aubyn, op. cit., p. 447.

23 Weintraub, op. cit. (*Victoria*), p. 452.

24 Longford, op. cit., p. 565.

25 Hibbert, op. cit., p. 298.

26 George Earle Buckle, ed., *The Letters of Queen Victoria 1886–1901*, third series (John Murray, London, 1932), vol. 1, p. 31.

27 St Aubyn, op. cit., p. 522.

28 Jeffrey L. Lant, *Insubstantial Pageant: Ceremony and Confusion at Queen Victoria's Court* (Hamish Hamilton, London, 1979), p. 103.

29 Bullock, op. cit., p. 200.

30 Strachey, op. cit., p. 170.

31 RA VIC/MAIN/QVJ/1878: 31 Dec.

32 Weintraub, op. cit. (*Victoria*), p. 391.

33 Lant, op. cit., p. 14.

34 Hugh Roberts, *The Queen's Diamonds* (Royal Collection, London, 2012), p. 70.

35 Longford, op. cit., p. 497.

36 Hibbert, op. cit., p. 299.

37 Ibid., p. 307.

38 Lant, op. cit., p. 152.

39 Hibbert, op. cit., p. 305.

40 Ibid., p. 305, p. 304.

41 Richard Williams, op. cit., p. 215.

42 Richard Hough, *Advice to a Granddaughter: Letters from Queen Victoria to Princess Victoria of Hesse* (Heinemann, London, 1975), p. 91.

43 Sophie Gordon, *Noble Hounds and Dear Companions* (Royal Collection Publications, London, 2007), p. 40.

CHAPTER ELEVEN

1 Buckle, ed., op. cit. (third series), vol. 3, p. 79.

2 Richard Williams, op. cit., p. 251.

3 St Aubyn, op. cit., p. 551.

4 Richard Williams, op. cit., p. 173.

5 Longford, op. cit., p. 558.

6 Hibbert, op. cit., p. 308.

7 Theo Aronson, *Heart of a Queen: Queen Victoria's Romantic Attachments* (John Murray, London, 1991), p. 234.

8 Van der Kiste, op. cit., p. 152.

9 Longford, op. cit., p. 575.

10 Arnstein, op. cit., p. 181.

11 Aronson, op. cit. (*Heart of a Queen*), p. 235.

12 John Matson, *Dear Osborne* (Hamish Hamilton, London, 1978), p. 104.

13 Van der Kiste, op. cit., p. 160.

14 Strachey, op. cit., p. 258.

15 *London Gazette*, 15 February 1896.

16 Hibbert, op. cit., p. 320.

17 Hubbard, op. cit., p. 293.

18 St Aubyn, op. cit., p. 491.

19 Arnstein, op. cit., p. 188.

20 Roberts, op. cit., p. 43.

21 Hibbert, op. cit., p. 335.

22 Richard Williams, op. cit., p. 177.

23 Ibid., p. 176.

24 St Aubyn, op. cit., p. 286.

25 Dyson and Tennyson, eds, op. cit., p. 148.

BIBLIOGRAPHY

Aldous, Richard, *The Lion and the Unicorn: Gladstone vs Disraeli* (Hutchinson, London, 2006)

Almedingen, E. A., *The Empress Alexandra* (Hutchinson, London, 1961)

Arengo-Jones, Peter, *Queen Victoria in Switzerland* (Robert Hale, London, 1995)

Arnstein, Walter L., *Queen Victoria* (Palgrave Macmillan, Basingstoke, 2003)

Aronson, Theo, *Queen Victoria and the Bonapartes* (Cassell, London, 1972)

————*Grandmama of Europe* (John Murray paperback, London, 1984)

————*Heart of a Queen: Queen Victoria's Romantic Attachments* (John Murray, London, 1991)

Auchincloss, Louis, *Persons of Consequence: Queen Victoria and Her Circle* (Weidenfeld & Nicolson, London, 1979)

Bagehot, Walter (ed. Miles Taylor), *The English Constitution* (Oxford World Classics reprint, Oxford, 2009)

Barthez, Dr E., *The Empress Eugenie and Her Circle* (T. Fisher Unwin, London, 1912)

Battiscombe, Georgina, *Queen Alexandra* (Constable, London, 1969)

Bennett, Daphne, *King without a Crown* (Heinemann, London, 1977)

——————*Queen Victoria's Children* (Gollancz, London, 1980)

Benson, E. F., *The Kaiser and English Relations* (Longmans, London, 1936)

——————*Daughters of Queen Victoria* (Cassell and Company, London, 1939)

Bessborough, Earl of, *Lady Charlotte Schreiber, Extracts from Her Journal 1853–1891* (John Murray, London, 1952)

Brett, Maurice V., ed., *Journals and Letters of Reginald Viscount Esher* (Ivor Nicholson & Watson, London, 1934)

Brown, Ivor, *Balmoral: The History of a Home* (Collins, London, 1955)

Buckle, George Earle, ed., *The Letters of Queen Victoria 1879–85*, second series (John Murray, London, 1928)

——————*The Letters of Queen Victoria 1886–1901*, third series (John Murray, London, 1932)

Bullock, Rev. Charles, *The Queen's Resolve: A Jubilee Memorial* (Home Words Publishing, London, 1887)

Cannizzo, Jeanne, *Our Highland Home: Victoria and Albert in Scotland* (National Galleries of Scotland, Edinburgh, 2005)

Clark, Ronald W., *Balmoral: Queen Victoria's Highland Home* (Thames & Hudson, London, 1981)

Creston, Dormer, *The Youthful Queen Victoria* (Macmillan & Co., London, 1952)

Cullen, Tom, *The Empress Brown: The Story of a Royal Friendship* (The Bodley Head, London, 1969)

De-la-Noy, Michael, *Queen Victoria at Home* (Constable & Robinson, London, 2003)

Dennison, Matthew, *The Last Princess: The Devoted Life of Queen Victoria's Youngest Daughter* (Weidenfeld & Nicolson, London, 2007)

Downer, Martyn, *The Queen's Knight* (Bantam Press, London, 2007)

Duff, David, *The Shy Princess* (Evans Brothers, London, 1958)

――――――*Hessian Tapestry* (Frederick Muller, London, 1967)

――――――*Victoria Travels: Journeys of Queen Victoria Between 1830 and 1900, with Extracts from Her Journal* (Frederick Muller, London, 1970)

――――――*Edward of Kent* (Frederick Muller reprint, London, 1973)

Dyson, Hope, and Tennyson, Charles, eds., *Dear and Honoured Lady: The Correspondence Between Queen Victoria and Alfred Tennyson* (Macmillan, London, 1969)

Epton, Nina, *Victoria and Her Daughters* (Weidenfeld & Nicolson, London, 1971)

Erbach-Schönberg, Princess Marie zu, Princess of Battenberg, *Reminiscences* (Royalty Digest reprint, Ticehurst, 1996)

Erickson, Carolly, *Her Little Majesty: The Life of Queen Victoria* (Robson Books, London, 1997)

Feuchtwanger, Edgar, *Albert and Victoria: The Rise and Fall of the House of Saxe-Coburg-Gotha* (Hambledon Continuum, London, 2006)

Field, Leslie, *The Queen's Jewels* (Weidenfeld & Nicolson, London, 1987)

Fraser, Flora, *Princesses: The Six Daughters of George III* (John Murray, London, 2004)

Fulford, Roger, *Queen Victoria* (Collins, London, 1951)

Fulford, Roger, ed., *Dearest Child: Letters from Queen Victoria and the Princess Royal, 1858–1861* (Evans Brothers, London, 1964)

――――――*Dearest Mama: Letters Between Queen Victoria and the Crown Princess of Prussia 1861–64* (Evans Brothers, London, 1968)

——————*Your Dear Letter: Private Correspondence of Queen Victoria and the Crown Princess of Prussia, 1856–71* (Evans Brothers, London, 1971)

——————*Darling Child: Private Correspondence of Queen Victoria and the Crown Princess of Prussia, 1871–78* (Evans Brothers, London, 1976)

——————*Beloved Mama: Private Correspondence of Queen Victoria and the German Crown Princess, 1878–85* (Evans Brothers, London, 1981)

Gelardi, Julia, *Born to Rule* (St Martin's Press, New York, 2004)

Gernsheim, Helmut and Alison, *Queen Victoria* (Longmans, Green and Co., London, 1959)

Gilmartin, Sophie, *Ancestry and Narrative in Nineteenth-Century British Literature: Blood Relations from Edgeworth to Hardy* (CUP paperback, Cambridge, 2005)

Gordon, Sophie, *Noble Hounds and Dear Companions* (Royal Collection Publications, London, 2007)

Grihange, Roger (trans. David Lockie), *Queen Victoria in Grasse* (Imprimerie Magenta, 1991)

Hibbert, Christopher, *Edward VII: A Portrait* (Allen Lane, London, 1976)

——————*George III: A Personal History* (Viking, London, 1998)

——————*Queen Victoria: A Personal History* (HarperCollins, London, 2000)

——————*Disraeli: A Personal History* (HarperCollins, London, 2004)

Hibbert, Christopher, ed., *Queen Victoria in Her Letters and Journals* (Viking, New York, 1985)

Homans, Margaret, and Munich, Adrienne, eds., *Remaking Queen Victoria* (Cambridge University Press, Cambridge, 1997)

Hough, Richard, *Advice to a Granddaughter: Letters from

Queen Victoria to Princess Victoria of Hesse (Heinemann, London, 1975)

——————*Edward & Alexandra: Their Private and Public Lives* (Hodder & Stoughton, London, 1993)

Housman, Laurence, *Happy and Glorious: A Dramatic Biography* (The Reprint Society, London, 1943)

Houston, Gail Turley, *Royalties: The Queen and Victorian Writers* (University Press of Virginia, Charlottesville and London, 1999)

Howard McClintock, Mary, *The Queen Thanks Sir Howard* (John Murray, London, 1945)

Hubbard, Kate, *Serving Victoria: Life in the Royal Household* (Chatto & Windus, London, 2012)

Hudson, Katherine, *A Royal Conflict: Sir John Conroy and the Young Victoria* (Hodder & Stoughton, London, 1994)

Hudson, W. H., *Birds in London* (Longmans, Green and Co., London, 1898)

Impey, Edward, *Kensington Palace: The Official Illustrated History* (Merrell, London, 2003)

Jagow, Dr Kurt, *Letters of the Prince Consort 1831–1861* (John Murray, London, 1938)

Jenkins, Roy, *Gladstone* (Macmillan, London, 1995)

Johnson, Malcolm, *Bustling Intermeddler? The Life and Work of Charles James Blomfield* (Gracewing paperback, Leominster, 2001)

Kuhn, William H., *Henry and Mary Ponsonby: Life at the Court of Queen Victoria* (Duckworth, London, 2002)

Lamont-Brown, Raymond, *John Brown, Queen Victoria's Highland Servant* (Sutton, Stroud, 2000)

Lant, Jeffrey L., *Insubstantial Pageant: Ceremony and Confusion at Queen Victoria's Court* (Hamish Hamilton, London, 1979)

Lee, Sidney, *King Edward VII* (Macmillan, London, 1925)

Longford, Elizabeth, *Victoria RI* (Weidenfeld & Nicolson, London, 1964)

Longford, Elizabeth, ed., *Louisa, Lady-in-Waiting* (Jonathan Cape, London, 1979)

——————ed., *Darling Loosy: Letters to Princess Louise 1856–1939* (Weidenfeld & Nicolson, London, 1991)

Lutyens, Mary, ed., *Lady Lytton's Diary* (Rupert Hart-Davis, London, 1961)

Magnus, Philip, *King Edward VII* (John Murray, London, 1964)

Mallet, Victor, ed., *Life with Queen Victoria: Marie Mallet's Letters from Court, 1887–1901* (John Murray, London, 1968)

Marie Louise, Princess, *My Memories of Six Reigns* (Evans Brothers, London, 1956)

Marsden, Jonathan, ed., *Victoria and Albert: Art and Love* (Royal Collections Publications, London, 2010)

Marshall, Dorothy, *The Life and Times of Queen Victoria* (Weidenfeld & Nicolson, London, 1972)

Martin, Theodore, *Queen Victoria As I Knew Her* (William Blackwood and Sons, Edinburgh and London, 1908)

Matson, John, *Dear Osborne* (Hamish Hamilton, London, 1978)

Menkes, Suzy, *The Royal Jewels* (Grafton Books, London, 1985)

Meylan, Vincent, *Queens' Jewels* (Assouline, New York, 2002)

Millar, Oliver, *The Victorian Paintings in the Collection of Her Majesty the Queen* (Cambridge University Press, Cambridge, 1992)

Munn, Geoffrey, *Tiaras: A History of Splendour* (Antique Collectors' Club, Woodbridge, 2001)

Murphy, Paul Thomas, *Shooting Victoria: Madness, Mayhem and the Modernisation of the Monarchy* (Head of Zeus, London, 2012)

Murray, Venetia, *High Society in the Regency Period* (Penguin, London, 1999)

Nelson, Michael, *Queen Victoria and the Discovery of the Riviera* (I. B. Tauris, London, 2001)

Noel, Gerard, *Princess Alice: Queen Victoria's Forgotten Daughter* (Constable, London, 1974)

——————*Ena: Spain's English Queen* (Constable, London, 1984)

Oliphant, Mrs, *Queen Victoria: A Personal Sketch* (Cassell and Company, London, 1901)

Packard, Jerrold M., *Queen Victoria's Daughters* (St Martin's Press, New York, 1998)

——————*Farewell in Splendour: The Death of Queen Victoria and Her Age* (Sutton, Stroud, 2000)

Pakula, Hannah, *An Uncommon Woman: The Empress Frederick* (Phoenix paperback, London, 1997)

Parissien, Steven, *George IV, The Grand Entertainment* (John Murray, London, 2001)

Paxman, Jeremy, *The Victorians: Britain through the Paintings of the Age* (BBC Books, London, 2009)

Plunkett, John, *Queen Victoria, First Media Monarch* (Oxford University Press, Oxford, 2003)

Ponsonby, Arthur, *Henry Ponsonby, Queen Victoria's Private Secretary: His Life from His Letters* (Macmillan & Co., London, 1943)

Ponsonby, Frederick, *Recollections of the Three Reigns* (Eyre & Spottiswoode, London, 1951)

Ponsonby, Frederick, ed., *Letters of the Empress Frederick* (Macmillan, London, 1928)

Ponsonby, Magdalen, ed., *Mary Ponsonby: A Memoir, Some Letters and a Journal* (John Murray, London, 1927)

Pope-Hennessy, James, *Queen Mary* (Allen & Unwin, London, 1959)

Pope-Hennessy, James, ed., *Queen Victoria at Windsor and*

Balmoral: Letters from Her Granddaughter Princess Victoria of Prussia June 1889 (George Allen & Unwin, London, 1959)

Ramm, Agatha, ed., *Beloved and Darling Child: Last Letters Between Queen Victoria and Her Eldest Daughter 1886–1901* (Sutton, Stroud, 1990)

Rappaport, Helen, *Queen Victoria: A Biographical Companion* (ABC Clio, 2003)

——————*Magnificent Obsession: Victoria, Albert and the Death that Changed the Monarchy* (Hutchinson, London, 2011)

Raymond, John, ed., *Queen Victoria's Early Letters* (Batsford, London, 1963)

Reid, Michaela, *Ask Sir James* (Hodder & Stoughton, London, 1987)

Rennell, Tony, *Last Days of Glory: The Death of Queen Victoria* (Viking, London, 2000)

Reynolds, K. D., and Matthew, H. C. G., *Queen Victoria* (Oxford University Press, Oxford, 2007)

Ridley, Jane, *Bertie: A Life of Edward VII* (Chatto & Windus, London, 2012)

Roberts, Hugh, *The Queen's Diamonds* (Royal Collection, London, 2012)

Roberts, Jane, *Royal Artists from Mary Queen of Scots to the Present Day* (Grafton Books, London, 1987)

Robinson, John Martin, *Windsor Castle* (Michael Joseph, London, 1996)

Rowell, George, *Queen Victoria Goes to the Theatre* (Paul Elek, London, 1978)

St Aubyn, Giles, *Edward VII Prince and King* (Collins, London, 1979)

——————*Queen Victoria: A Portrait* (Sinclair Stevenson, London, 1991)

St-John Nevill, Barry, *Life at the Court of Queen Victoria 1861–1901* (Webb & Bower, Exeter, 1984)

Sheppard, Edgar, *Memorials of St James's Palace* (Longmans, Green and Co., London, 1894)

Sinclair, Andrew, *The Other Victoria: The Princess Royal and the Great Game of Europe* (Weidenfeld & Nicolson, London, 1981)

Steuart Erskine, Mrs, ed., *Twenty Years at Court: From the Correspondence of the Hon. Eleanor Stanley, 1842–62* (Nisbet & Co., London, 1916)

Stoney, Benita, and Weltzein, Heinrich C., *My Mistress the Queen: The Letters of Frieda Arnold, Dresser to Queen Victoria, 1854–59*, trans. by Sheila de Bellaigue (Weidenfeld & Nicolson, London, 1994)

Stothard, Jane T., *The Life of the Empress Eugenie* (Hodder & Stoughton, London, 1906)

Strachey, Lytton, *Queen Victoria* (Chatto & Windus reprint, London, 1928)

Stuart, D. M., *Daughter of England* (Macmillan & Co., London, 1951)

Thomson, David, *England in the Nineteenth Century* (Penguin reprint, London, 1986)

Tisdall, E. E. P., *Queen Victoria's Private Life* (Jarrolds, London, 1961)

Vallone, Lynne, *Becoming Victoria* (Yale University Press, 2001)

Van der Kiste, John, *Queen Victoria's Children* (Sutton, Stroud, 1986)

————*Edward VII's Children* (Sutton, Stroud, 1989)

————*George V's Children* (Sutton, Stroud, 1991)

————*George III's Children* (Sutton, Stroud, 1992)

————*Sons, Servants and Statesmen: The Men in Queen Victoria's Life* (Sutton, Stroud, 2006)

Vickers, Hugo, *Alice, Princess Andrew of Greece* (Viking, London, 2000)

Victoria, Queen, *Leaves from the Journal of Our Life in the*

Highlands: From 1848 to 1861 (Smith, Elder & Co., London, 1868)

——————*More Leaves from the Journal of Our Life in the Highlands: From 1862 to 1882* (Smith, Elder & Co., London, 1884)

Wake, Jehanne, *Princess Louise: Queen Victoria's Unconventional Daughter* (London, Collins, 1988)

Ward, Yvonne M., *Editing Queen Victoria: How Men of Letters Constructed the Young Queen* (PhD thesis, La Trobe University, Australia, 2004)

Warner, Marina, *Queen Victoria's Sketchbook* (Macmillan, London, 1979)

Watson, Vera, *A Queen at Home: An Intimate Account of the Social and Domestic Life of Queen Victoria's Court* (W. H. Allen, London, 1952)

Weintraub, Stanley, *Victoria: Biography of a Queen* (Unwin, London, 1987)

——————*Albert Uncrowned King* (John Murray paperback, London, 1998)

Williams, Kate, *Becoming Queen* (Hutchinson, London, 2008)

Williams, Richard, *The Contentious Crown: Public Discussion of the British Monarchy in the Reign of Queen Victoria* (Ashgate, Aldershot, 1997)

Windsor, Dean of, and Bolitho, Hector, eds., *Letters of Lady Augusta Stanley* (George Howe, London, 1927)

——————*Later Letters of Lady Augusta Stanley* (Jonathan Cape, London, 1929)

Woodham-Smith, Cecil, *Victoria 1819–1861* (Hamish Hamilton, London, 1972)

Zeepvat, Charlotte, *Prince Leopold: The Untold Story of Queen Victoria's Youngest Son* (Sutton, Stroud, 1988)

INDEX

INDEX